Katharina Walter
Claudine Steyer

Englisch üben

Differenzierte Materialien
für das ganze Schuljahr

5

Auer

Die Vorlagen auf CD sind optimiert für Microsoft Office 2007 SPXX basierend auf Windows 7®.

Gedruckt auf umweltbewusst gefertigtem, chlorfrei gebleichtem und alterungsbeständigem Papier.

4. Auflage 2020
Nach den seit 2006 amtlich gültigen Regelungen der Rechtschreibung
© Auer Verlag
AAP Lehrerwelt GmbH, Augsburg
Alle Rechte vorbehalten
Das Werk und seine Teile sind urheberrechtlich geschützt. Jede Nutzung in anderen als den gesetzlich zugelassenen Fällen bedarf der vorherigen schriftlichen Einwilligung des Verlages.
Hinweis zu § 52 a UrhG: Weder das Werk noch seine Teile dürfen ohne eine solche Einwilligung eingescannt und in ein Netzwerk eingestellt werden. Dies gilt auch für Intranets von Schulen und sonstigen Bildungseinrichtungen.
Umschlagfoto: Fotolia
Illustrationen: Steffen Jähde, Hendrik Kranenberg
Satz: Typographie & Computer, Krefeld
Druck und Bindung: Himmer GmbH, Augsburg
CD-Pressung: optimal media production GmbH, Hamburg
ISBN 978-3-403-**06603**-3

www.auer-verlag.de

Inhaltsverzeichnis

Vorwort 4

Present progressive 5
    Statements 5
    Negation 8
    Questions 11

Simple present 14
    Statements – to do/to be 14
    Negation – to do/to be 17
    Questions – to do/to be 20
    Statements – have got 23
    Negation – have got 26
    Questions – have got 29

Going to-future 32
    Statements 32
    Negation 35
    Questions 38

At school 41
    The classroom 41
    Lessons 44
    Numbers 47
    Time 50
    Timetable 55
    Prepositions 56

At home 59
    Family members 59
    Our house 62
    Sports and hobbies 65
    Animals and pets 68
    S-genitive 71
    Food and drinks 74
    Body parts and clothes 77
    Colours 81

Pronouns and question words 84
    Personal pronouns 84
    Possessive pronouns 87
    Object pronouns 90
    Question words 93

Die Lösungen zu allen Aufgaben finden Sie auf der beiliegenden CD-ROM.

Vorwort

Schüler[1] individuell zu fördern, bedeutet, sie da abzuholen, wo sie stehen. Konkret heißt das, dass bereits vorhandene Kompetenzen gezielt ausgebaut werden. Um diesem Anspruch gerecht zu werden, sollten Übungsmaterialien entsprechend unterschiedliche Schwierigkeitsstufen bedienen.

In der vorliegenden Unterrichtshilfe finden Sie zu **sechs grundlegenden Themen des 5. Schuljahrs**, die noch einmal in Unterthemen aufgegliedert sind, **Arbeitsblätter auf zwei Niveaustufen**. Zusätzlich gibt es zu Beginn jedes Unterthemas ein **Merkblatt**, mit dem Sie noch einmal die wichtigsten Inhalte wiederholen können. Folgende Themen werden behandelt:

- Present progressive,
- Simple present,
- Going-to-future,
- At school,
- At home,
- Pronouns and question words.

Alle Blätter sind in den Kopfzeilen entsprechend ihrer Einsatzmöglichkeit oder ihres Schwierigkeitsgrades gekennzeichnet: (i) für die Merkblätter, für die leichten Arbeitsblätter, für die schwereren.

Die Aufgaben auf jedem Arbeitsblatt wurden nach dem Prinzip **„vom Leichten zum Schweren"** erstellt. So können sowohl schnellere als auch langsamere Schüler adäquat und effektiv gefördert werden. Im Sinne eines produktiven Übens fördern die Materialien das automatisierende Üben (Fertigkeiten einüben), das operative Üben (Zusammenhänge erkennen), das problemorientierte Üben (Problemlösestrategien entwickeln) und das anwendungsorientierte Üben (Bezug zur Lebenspraxis).

Das entsprechende Merkblatt kann als Folie (zur gemeinsamen Besprechung im Unterricht) oder als Kopiervorlage verwendet werden. Neben einer kurzen Zusammenfassung der wesentlichen Inhalte finden Sie hier z. B. Definitionen und wichtige Merkregeln.

Alle Aufgaben aus dem Buch sowie die vollständigen Lösungen finden Sie in veränderbarer Form auf der beiliegenden **CD-ROM**, d. h. Sie können alle Aufgaben noch einmal individuell auf Ihre jeweilige Lerngruppe zuschneiden, nach Belieben Aufgaben weglassen oder ergänzen usw.

Zur Diagnose und Lernstandsüberprüfung empfehlen wir Ihnen die Bände **„Auer Führerscheine Englisch Klasse 5"** (Bestell-Nr. 6721) und **„Klassenarbeiten Englisch 5"** (Bestell-Nr. 6723). Beide Unterrichtshilfen sind nach demselben Inhaltsverzeichnis wie der vorliegende Band konzipiert. Sie können also mit dem kompletten Programm „Auer Führerscheine Englisch", „Englisch üben" und „Klassenarbeiten Englisch" schnell und einfach die Kompetenzen Ihrer Schüler diagnostizieren, entsprechende Materialien zum Üben anbieten und in einer Klassenarbeit abfragen.

Die drei Bände eignen sich somit hervorragend, um einen entsprechenden Förderplan mit genauer Angabe der Stärken und Defizite sowie der Fördermöglichkeiten zu erstellen und ggf. auch an die Eltern weiterzureichen.

Viel Erfolg bei der Arbeit mit den Materialien wünschen Ihnen

Claudine Steyer und Katharina Walter

---

[1] Wenn in diesem Buch von Schüler gesprochen wird, ist immer auch die Schülerin gemeint. Ebenso verhält es sich mit Lehrer und Lehrerin.

Statements

Die Verwendung des Present Progressive

Das Present Progressive ist eine Zeitform, die
- ausdrückt, was gerade im Moment geschieht.
- ausdrücken kann, was in naher Zukunft geschehen wird.

Du verwendest es immer dann, wenn du
- sagen möchtest, was jemand **gerade** tut / was **gerade** passiert.
  (Beispiel: *Look, the dog is running after a rabbit.*)
- **Bilder** beschreibst.
  (Beispiel: *I can see a girl. She is eating an ice cream.*)
- ausdrücken möchtest, was jemand **in naher Zukunft** tun wird **(Plan)**.
  (Beispiel: *She is coming tomorrow.*)

Die Bildung des Present Progressive

Du bildest das Present Progressive so:
Form von *to be* (am, are, is) + **Verb im Infinitiv** + **-ing**
  (Beispiel: *I am going, he is playing …*)

Vorsicht:
- endet das Verb auf „m / n / p / t" nach kurzem Vokal, verdoppelt sich der Konsonant.
  (Beispiel: *swim – swimming.* So z. B. auch bei *hit, run, step, cut …*)
- endet das Verb auf „e", fällt dieses „e" weg.
  (Beispiel: *come – coming.* So z. B. auch bei *ride, become, skate …*)

Kurzformen

Du kannst auch **Kurzformen** verwenden:
1. *I **am** doing my homework.* → *I**'m** doing my homework.*
2. *He **is** reading a book.* → *He**'s** reading a book.*
3. *They **are** waiting for the bus.* → *They**'re** waiting for the bus.*

Signalwörter

An folgenden **Signalwörtern** kannst du das Present Progressive erkennen:
- gerade, im Moment: *Look, listen, now, at the moment, right now*
- in naher Zukunft *tomorrow, soon, in a moment, in 5 minutes …*

Statements

1. Fill in the matching form of "be".

a) 1. Pers. Sing.   I   _____ listening

b) 2. Pers. Sing.   you   _____ listening

c) 3. Pers. Sing.   he / she / it   _____ listening

d) 1. Pers. Pl.   we   _____ listening

e) 2. Pers. Pl.   you   _____ listening

f) 3. Pers. Pl.   they   _____ listening

2. Put the sentences into the correct order.

a) is / to the radio / Betty / listening
b) football / the boys / playing / are
c) sleeping / in its cage / is / the rabbit
d) my bike / I / repairing / am
e) raining / it / is
f) our homework / doing / are / we

3. Fill in the present progressive form of the verb.

a) Sue (meet) Cathy in the park now.
b) I (help) my mum in the garden.
c) The friends (watch) a quiz on TV.
d) My brother (play) with our dog.
e) We (tidy up) our rooms at the moment.
f) You (listen) to your new CD.

4. Write correct sentences. Use the present progressive.

a) Robert / read / a comic
b) Susan and Sarah / prepare / lunch
c) I / do / my homework

5. Translate the sentences into English. Use the present progressive.

a) Die Familie isst zurzeit Abendbrot.
b) Sie liest gerade ein neues Buch.
c) Ich füttere im Moment die Katze.

6. Use the short form of the present progressive.

a) I am preparing breakfast for my family.
b) The team is winning the match.
c) They are meeting at the bus stop.
d) She is waiting for her friend.

Present progressive

Statements

1. **Write down the correct form of the verb in the present progressive.**

   a) 1. Pers. Sing.   I (sing)
   b) 2. Pers. Sing.   you (sing
   c) 3. Pers. Sing.   he / she / it (sing)
   d) 1. Pers. Pl.   we (sing)
   e) 2. Pers. Pl.   you (sing)
   f) 3. Pers. Pl.   they (sing)

2. **Fill in the present progressive form of the verb.**

   a) Cathy (walk) her dog in the park now.
   b) I (watch) the birds in the garden.
   c) The friends (play) a game in Tom's room.
   d) My sister (read) a book in the living room.
   e) We (clean) our rooms at the moment.
   f) You (eat) a tasty sandwich.

3. **Write down the sentences in the present progressive. Use the short form if possible.**

   a) Robert / draw / a picture
   b) Susan and Sarah / eat / lunch
   c) I / go / to bed
   d) We / play / a new computer game
   e) You / sit / on my chair
   f) The teacher / tell / a story

4. **Answer the questions in the present progressive.**

   a) What is Sam repairing? – Sam / repair / his bike
   b) Where is Sue waiting? – Sue / wait / at the cinema
   c) What are they eating? – They / eat / pizza

5. **Put the sentences into the correct order. Underline the signal words.**

   a) play / David / his guitar / listen
   b) I / my homework / at the moment / do

6. **Translate the following sentences. Use the present progressive and the short form if possible.**

   a) Schau, der Bus kommt!
   b) Ich füttere das Kaninchen.
   c) Meine Freunde spielen im Park.
   d) Betty fährt Fahrrad.

Present progressive

Negation

Die Verwendung des Present Progressive

Das Present Progressive ist eine Zeitform, die
- ausdrückt, was gerade im Moment (nicht) geschieht.
- ausdrücken kann, was in naher Zukunft (nicht) geschehen wird.

Du verwendest es immer dann, wenn du
- sagen möchtest, was jemand **gerade** nicht tut.
  (Beispiel: *Look, the dog isn't running after the rabbit.*)
- **Bilder** beschreibst.
  (Beispiel: *I can see a girl. She isn't eating an ice cream.*)
- ausdrücken möchtest, was jemand **in naher Zukunft** nicht tun wird (**Plan**). (Beispiel: *She's not coming tomorrow.*)

Die Bildung der Verneinung im Present Progressive

Du bildest die Verneinung im Present Progressive, indem du „**not**" hinter das Hilfsverb stellst.

Form von *to be (am, are, is)* + not + Infinitiv + *-ing*

(Beispiel: *I am **not** going, he is **not** playing …*)

Kurzformen

In der Verneinung verwendest du fast immer **Kurzformen**:

1. *I **am not** doing my homework.* → *I'**m not** doing my homework.*
2. *He **is not** reading a book.* → *He **isn't** reading a book.*
3. *They **are not** waiting for the bus.* → *They **aren't** waiting for the bus.*

Negation

1. a. Tick the correct negations in the present progressive.
   b. Correct the other sentences with the right negative form in the present progressive.

   a) Tom is not reading a comic. ☐
   b) Sarah and Betty going not to the cinema. ☐
   c) I am not doing my homework. ☐
   d) We do not watch a quiz on TV. ☐
   e) They are not playing in the garden. ☐

2. Put the following sentences into the correct order.

   a) is / to a CD / Lily / not / listening
   b) hockey / not / the girls / playing / are
   c) not / sleeping / in its basket / is / the dog
   d) my room / I / tidying up / am / not
   e) snowing / it / not / is
   f) our homework / doing / not / are / we

3. Write down the negative statements in the present progressive.

   a) Chloe is waiting for Emily in the park.
   b) I am helping my dad in the garden.
   c) The children are watching TV.
   d) My sister is playing with her rabbit.
   e) We are doing our homework.
   f) You are reading your new book.

4. Write down the negative statements. Use the present progressive.

   a) Jack / read / a comic
   b) Olivia and Sarah / prepare / lunch
   c) I / do / my homework

5. Write down the sentences in the short form.

   a) I am not preparing lunch.
   b) My family is not going on holiday.
   c) You are not meeting your friend on the playground.
   d) She is not writing an e-mail.
   e) They are not listening to the radio.
   f) I am not working on my computer.

6. Translate the following sentences in the present progressive. Use the short form.

   a) Harry schläft nicht.
   b) Wir spielen nicht in meinem Zimmer.
   c) Ich singe nicht im Chor.

Negation

1. Underline the correct negative form in the present progressive.

a) Susan and Jake don't play / aren't playing tennis at the beach at the moment.
b) "Listen, Daniel doesn't play / isn't playing the drums in his room. He's sleeping."
c) "Look, Tom's rabbits don't eat / aren't eating carrots. Aren't they hungry?"
d) "Ok Mum, I can help you. I don't do / I'm not doing my homework right now."

2. Correct the following sentences with the matching negative form.

a) I read not my favourite book.
b) Sophie and Ruby going not to the cinema.
c) We do not watch a quiz on TV.

3. Write down the negative statements. Use the short form.

a) I am not preparing lunch.
b) My family is not going on holiday.
c) You are not meeting your friend on the playground.

4. Write down the negative sentences.

a) The cat is sleeping on the sofa.
b) Jake is playing the guitar.
c) Tom is doing his homework.
d) We are eating ice cream.
e) The children are running home.

5. Write down the negative statements in the present progressive.

a) Joshua / learn / for his Maths test
b) Jessica and Grace / preparing / dinner
c) I / listen / to a great CD
d) We / sing / our favourite song

6. Write down negative statements in the present progressive and use the short form.

	activity	no
a)	Evie / do her homework	X
b)	Thomas and Charlie / clean their bikes	X
c)	The children / learn Spanish at school	X
d)	I / have breakfast with James	X

7. Translate the sentences. Use the present progressive and the short form.

a) Wiliam hilft nicht im Garten.
b) Ich treffe mich nicht mit meinen Freunden.
c) Sie gehen nicht gemeinsam ins Kino.

Questions

Die Verwendung des Present Progressive

Das Present Progressive ist eine Zeitform, die
- ausdrückt, was gerade im Moment geschieht.
- ausdrücken kann, was in naher Zukunft geschehen wird.

Du verwendest es immer dann, wenn du
- erfragen möchtest, was jemand **gerade** tut / was **gerade** passiert.
  (Beispiel: *Look, is the dog running after a rabbit?*)
- Fragen zu **Bildern** stellst.
  (Beispiel: *Look at the girl. Is she eating an ice cream?*)
- erfragen möchtest, was jemand **in naher Zukunft** tun wird **(Plan)**.
  (Beispiel: *Is she coming tomorrow?*)

Die Bildung von Fragen im Present Progressive

Du kannst **2 Arten von Fragen** stellen und bilden:
1. Ja/Nein-Fragen (man kann nur mit ja oder nein antworten)
2. Fragen mit Fragewörtern

1. Ja/Nein-Fragen

Du vertauschst **Subjekt** und **Hilfsverb/Verb** des Aussagesatzes.

Aussage:	Susan	*is*	reading a comic.
Frage:	*Is*	Susan	reading a comic?

2. Fragen mit Fragewort

Du stellst ein **Fragewort** vor die Ja/Nein-Frage.

Ja/Nein-Frage:	*Is Susan reading a comic?*	
Fragewortfrage:	***What** is Susan reading?*	*A comic.*

Kurzantworten zu Ja/Nein-Fragen

Wenn du eine Ja/Nein-Frage beantworten möchtest, reicht meist eine **Kurzantwort**.

Beispiel: *Is David riding his bike?* → ***Yes, he is. / No, he isn't.***
Are they waiting for me? → ***Yes, they are. / No, they aren't.***

Questions

1. **Read the answers and put the questions into the correct order.**

   a) Q: the children / tidying up / are / their rooms?
      A: Yes, they are tidying up their rooms.

   b) Q: doing / George / is / his homework?
      A: No, he isn't doing his homework. He is sleeping.

   c) Q: against London / the team / playing / is?
      A: No, the team is playing against Nottingham.

   d) Q: coming / you / are / to my party?
      A: Yes, I am coming to your party.

   e) Q: she / listening / to her music / is?
      A: Yes, she is listening to her new CD.

2. **Write down yes/no-questions in the present progressive.**

   a) Cathy is riding her bike.
   b) The children are eating fish and chips.
   c) The team is meeting after school.
   d) Ethan is bringing his best friend.
   e) Charlotte and Carol are playing their favourite game.
   f) The cat is drinking milk.

3. **Write down yes/no-questions in the present progressive.**

   a) Amy / play / the leading role?
   b) David / wear / that silly hat?
   c) Katie / dance / in the first line?
   d) Oscar / play / his guitar / in the band?

4. **Read the answers and fill in the matching question word.**

who	where	when	how	why

   a) _____ are they meeting after school? – In the park.

   b) _____ are you tidying up your room? – At 4 o'clock.

   c) _____ is sitting next to Isabelle? – Megan.

   d) _____ is she feeling? – Oh, a lot better, thanks.

   e) _____ are we walking this way? – Because it's shorter.

5. **Ask for the underlined information. Write down questions with question words.**

   a) He's playing hockey.
   b) They're working in Ella's room.
   c) I'm riding the black horse.

Present progressive

Questions

1. **Read the answers then write down the questions.**

   a) Q: the boys / tidying up / are / the shed?
      A: Yes, they are tidying up the shed.

   b) Q: doing / Rob / is / sports?
      A: No, he isn't doing sports. He is sleeping.

   c) Q: against Nottingham / Chelsea / playing / is?
      A: No, Nottingham is playing against London.

   d) Q: coming / you / are / to the cinema?
      A: Yes, I am coming to the cinema.

   e) Q: she / listening / to her new CD / is?
      A: Yes, she is listening to it in her room just now.

2. **Write down yes/no-questions in the present progressive.**

   a) Daisy is riding her horse.
   b) The girls are eating pasta and salad.
   c) The choir is meeting after school.
   d) Ben is waiting for his best friend.
   e) Becky and Ava are watching their favourite film.

3. **Write down yes/no-questions in the present progressive.**

   a) Holly / play / the leading role?
   b) Lewis / wear / that silly costume?
   c) Ruby / stand / in the first line?
   d) Liam / play / the drums / in the band?
   e) The girls / sing / with a microphone?

4. **Read the answers and write down questions with the matching question word.**

who	where	when	how	why

   a) _____ they / meet / after school? – In the park.
   b) _____ you / tidy up / your room? – At 4 o'clock.
   c) _____ stand / next to Hannah? – Grace.
   d) _____ she / feel? – Oh, a lot better, thanks.
   e) _____ we / walk this way? – Because it's shorter.

5. **Ask for the missing information. Write down questions with question words.**

   a) He is singing _____. – …?
   b) They are playing in _____. – …?
   c) They are coming at _____. – …?
   d) _____ are playing in the band. – …?
   e) I am eating a _____. – …?

Present progressive 13

Statements – to do / to be

Die Verwendung des Simple Present

Das Simple Present ist eine Zeitform,
- die ausdrückt, was regelmäßig und häufig geschieht (Tagesabläufe ...).
- die unveränderliche Tatsachen ausdrückt (z. B. in der Natur).
- mit der du Informationen zu Personen, Dingen gibst (Alter, Name ...).

Du verwendest es immer dann, wenn du
- sagen möchtest, was jemand **regelmäßig** tut / was **häufig** passiert.
  (Beispiel: *She sings in a choir every Tuesday.*)
- eine **unveränderliche Tatsache** darstellst.
  (Beispiel: *Water boils at 100°C. / A bird comes from an egg.*)
- Dinge/Personen **beschreiben** möchtest.
  (Beispiel: *She is ten. / She comes from Spain. / She speaks Spanish.*)

Die Bildung des Simple Present

Du bildest das Simple Present mit dem Infinitiv des Verbs.
Bei der 3. Person Singular hängst du ein „s" an.

I	eat
you	eat
he/she/it	eat**s**
we	eat
you	eat
they	eat

Merksatz: „he, she, it – the ‚s' must fit"

Vorsicht:
- endet ein Verb auf „s" oder einen Zischlaut, hängt man **„es"** an.
  (Beispiel: *watch – watches, wash – washes*)
- endet ein Verb auf „y" nach einem Konsonanten, hängt man **„ies"** an.
  (Beispiel: *cry – cries, try – tries*)
- endet ein Verb mit „o", hängt man auch ein **„es"** an.
  (Beispiel: *go – goes, do – does*)

Signalwörter

Es gibt **Signalwörter**, die an festen Stellen im Satz stehen:
- **nach dem Subjekt:** *usually* (gewöhnlich), *always* (immer), *never* (nie), *often* (oft), *sometimes* (manchmal)
- **Satzanfang / Satzende:** *every...* (jeden ...), *on Mondays...* (montags ...)

Simple present

Statements – to do / to be

1. **Write down the verbs in the simple present.**

   a) I (sing)
   b) she (listen)
   c) we (eat)
   d) it (rain)
   e) you (read)
   f) he (write)
   g) the cat (drink)
   h) the boys (play)
   i) I (come)
   j) Phoebe (help)
   k) Millie and Freya (swim)
   l) Max (run)

2. **Underline the correct forms of "to be".**

   a) Noah are / is / am
   b) my mother am / are / is
   c) Lisa and Ryan is / am / are
   d) Erin and I am / are / is
   e) I is / are / am
   f) her dog are / is / am

3. **Write down the verbs in the simple present.**

   a) the cat (catch)
   b) my mum (wash)
   c) he (go)
   d) Dan (do)
   e) my little sister (cry)
   f) the plane (fly)

4. **Put the sentences into the correct order.**

   a) usually / Amanda / reads / comics / after school
   b) feeds / the hamster / never / Isabella
   c) sometimes / the children / meet / at Scarlett's house
   d) Dave / every Friday / plays chess / at school
   e) goes swimming / Luke / on Wednesdays

5. **Write down the following sentences with the correct verbs in the simple present.**

   a) Mrs Grey (be) my favourite Maths teacher.
   b) Sally the cat (catch) a mouse every morning.
   c) Megan and Amy (be) from London.
   d) Joseph (do) his homework at 5 o'clock.
   e) Jayden always (read) a comic before he goes to bed.
   f) The Richards (ride) their bikes on Sundays.

6. **Write down statements in the simple present. Put the signal words in the right position.**

   a) Riley / read / a book / sometimes
   b) June and Lily / prepare / lunch / usually
   c) I / do / my homework / every day
   d) often / the cat / on the sofa / sleep

Simple present

Statements – to do / to be

1. **Write down the verbs in the simple present.**

   a) I (learn)
   b) the girls (play)
   c) it (snow)
   d) Amy and Ella (ride)
   e) the cat (catch)
   f) we (eat)
   g) Betty (help)
   h) he (read)
   i) she (look)
   j) I (go)
   k) you (watch)
   l) David (jump)

2. **Write down the following sentences. Use the correct forms of "be".**

   a) Tom (be) a nice boy.
   b) I (be) good in English.
   c) Carol and I (be) best friends.
   d) Lucy and Danny (be) 10 years old.
   e) My dad (be) a great cook.
   f) Her cat (be) so cute.

3. **Write down full sentences in the simple present.**

   a) the dog (catch) / a cat
   b) he (eat) / a burger
   c) Archie (do) / it well
   d) my little brother (cry) / often
   e) my dad (watch) / TV
   f) the bird (fly) / over the tree

4. **Write down sentences in the simple present. Put the signal words in the correct position.**

   a) usually / Kate / read / a book / on Sundays
   b) feed / the guinea-pig / never / Harry
   c) sometimes / the girls / meet / in Poppy's room
   d) Rob / every Friday / play hockey / in the park
   e) go swimming / Ben / on Mondays

5. **Write down the following sentences in the simple present.**

   a) Mrs Smith (be) my favourite French teacher.
   b) Sammy the dog (run) after the rabbit every morning.
   c) Chloe and Emily (be) from York.
   d) Dave (go) to the park at 5 o'clock.
   e) Daniel always (read) a comic before he goes to sleep.
   f) The Carters (take) a walk on Sundays.

6. **Write down sentences in the simple present. Put the signal words in the correct position.**

   a) Robert / write / e-mails / sometimes
   b) Evie and Kelly / prepare / dinner / usually
   c) I / learn / the English vocabulary / every day
   d) often / the dog / under the sofa / sleep

7. **Write down statements in the simple present.**

	who?	what?	when?
a)	Carol	sing in the choir	every Tuesday
b)	Ruby and Mia	play hockey	on Sundays
c)	Liam	ride his bike to school	usually
d)	The team	meet on the playground	always

Simple present

Negation – to do / to be

Die Verwendung des Simple Present

Das Simple Present ist eine Zeitform,
- die ausdrückt, was regelmäßig und häufig geschieht (Tagesabläufe ...).
- die unveränderliche Tatsachen ausdrückt (z. B. in der Natur).
- mit der du Informationen zu Personen, Dingen gibst (Alter, Name ...).

Du verwendest es immer dann, wenn du
- sagen möchtest, was jemand **regelmäßig nicht** tut / was **häufig** nicht passiert.
  (Beispiel: *She doesn't sing in a choir every Tuesday.*)
- eine **unveränderliche Tatsache** darstellst.
  (Beispiel: *Water doesn't boil at 80 °C.*)
- Dinge / Personen **beschreiben** möchtest.
  (Beispiel: *She isn't ten. / I don't come from Spain. / I don't speak Spanish.*)

Die Bildung der Verneinung im Simple Present

a) Du verneinst im Simple Present mit dem **Hilfsverb „do"** und **„not"**.

I	do	not eat	
you	do	not eat	
he/she/it	**does**	not eat	**Merksatz: "he, she, it – the ,s' must fit"**
we	do	not eat	Die Merkregel darfst du bei der Verneinung
you	do	not eat	nur auf das Hilfsverb „do" anwenden!
they	do	not eat	Du darfst kein „s" an das Vollverb anhängen!

b) Du verneinst im Simple Present mit dem **Hilfsverb „be"** und **„not"**.

I	am not
you	are not
he/she/it	is not
we	are not
you	are not
they	are not

Kurzformen

In der Verneinung verwendest du fast immer **Kurzformen**:

I do not / I **don't**	she does not / she **doesn't**
you are not / you **aren't**	he is not / he **isn't**

Negation – to do / to be

1. **Tick the correct negative sentences in the simple present.**

    a) I doesn't sing a song. ☐
    b) The cat doesn't drink milk. ☐
    c) She listens not to the radio. ☐
    d) We aren't eating pasta. ☐
    e) Megan doesn't play hockey on Tuesdays. ☐
    f) The boys don't take the bus to school. ☐

2. **Write down the short forms.**

    a) Max does not
    b) my mother is not
    c) You do not
    d) Lisa and Jake do not
    e) Sophie and I are not
    f) our school is not
    g) I am not
    h) the rabbits are not
    i) Mia does not

3. **Write down the sentences. Fill in "isn't / aren't / 'm not".**

    a) David ... from England.
    b) We … 10 years old.
    c) I … good at Maths.
    d) She … my best friend.
    e) The girls … at home.
    f) You … blonde.
    g) I … in the drama group.

4. **Fill in "don't / doesn't" and write down the sentences.**

    a) Jenny … play basketball.
    b) The Carters … live in London.
    c) I … speak Spanish.
    d) Carrie and Miranda … listen to rock music.
    e) Charlotte … play an instrument in the school orchestra.
    f) You … play the guitar.
    g) The cat … drink coffee.
    h) Lessons … start at 7am.

5. **Write down negative statements in the simple present.**

    a) Olivia feeds the hamster.
    b) The children meet at Lucy's house.
    c) I play chess at school.
    d) We go swimming on Wednesdays.

6. **Write down full answers in the simple present. Use the long form for emphasis.**

    a) Is Mrs Grey your favourite Maths teacher? – No, ….
    b) Does Molly the cat catch a mouse every morning? – No, ….
    c) Are Charlotte and Samantha from London? – No, ….
    d) Does Dave do his homework at 5 o'clock? – No, ….
    e) Do they always eat cornflakes for breakfast? – No, ….

Simple present

Negation – to do / to be

1. **Tick the correct negative sentences in the simple present.**

    a) I doesn't read a book. ☐
    b) The dog doesn't drink coffee. ☐
    c) She listens not to the CD. ☐
    d) They aren't eating pizza. ☐
    e) Danny doesn't play tennis on Tuesdays. ☐
    f) The girls don't take their bikes to school. ☐

2. **Write down the negative short forms.**

    a) Kelly does not
    b) my sister is not
    c) I do not
    d) Holly and Max do not
    e) Phil and I are not
    f) our teacher is not
    g) I am not
    h) the cats are not
    i) Meredith does not

3. **Write down negative statements in the simple present.**

    a) Marc (be) from England.
    b) We (be) 10 years old.
    c) I (be) good at Maths.
    d) She (be) my best friend.
    e) The girls (be) at home.
    f) I (be) in the drama group.

4. **Write down negative sentences in the simple present.**

    a) Alice plays the piano.
    b) The Richards live in York.
    c) Ayla speaks Spanish.
    d) Christina and Kelly listen to pop music.
    e) Danny plays the flute in the school orchestra.
    f) You play the drums.
    g) The budgie drinks milk.
    h) School starts at 7am.

5. **Write full answers in the simple present. Use the long form for emphasis.**

    a) Is Mrs Smith your favourite English teacher? – No, ….
    b) Does Parker the dog run after a rabbit every morning? – No, ….
    c) Are Harry and Alex from Chester? – No, ….
    d) Does Grace do her presentation at 10 o'clock? – No, ….
    e) Do they always eat eggs for breakfast? – No, ….

6. **Write negative statements in the simple present.**

	who?	what?	when?
a)	Derek	play chess	on Mondays
b)	Lexie and her sister	drink cocoa for lunch	usually
c)	I	do my homework	every afternoon
d)	You	meet your friends	sometimes

Simple present

Questions – to do / to be

Die Verwendung des Simple Present

Das Simple Present ist eine Zeitform,
- die ausdrückt, was regelmäßig und häufig geschieht (Tagesabläufe ...).
- die unveränderliche Tatsachen ausdrückt (z. B. in der Natur).
- mit der du Informationen zu Personen, Dingen gibst (Alter, Name ...).

Du verwendest es immer dann, wenn du
- erfragen möchtest, was jemand **regelmäßig** tut / was **häufig** passiert.
  (Beispiel: *Does she sing in a choir every Tuesday?*)
- eine **unveränderliche Tatsache** erfragst.
  (Beispiel: *Does water boil at 100 °C? / Does a bird come from an egg?*)
- **Informationen** über Dinge/Personen **erfragen** möchtest.
  (Beispiel: *Is she ten? / Where does she come from?*)

Die Bildung des Simple Present

Du kannst **2 Arten von Fragen** stellen und bilden:
1. Ja/Nein-Fragen (man kann nur mit ja oder nein antworten)
2. Fragen mit Fragewörtern

1. Ja/Nein-Fragen

a. Hilfsverb „do"

Form von	„do"	+	Subjekt	+	Vollverb
Beispiel:	Does	+	Susan	+	sing ...

b. Hilfsverb „be"

Form von	„be"	+	Subjekt
Beispiel:	Is	+	Susan ...

2. Fragen mit Fragewort

Du stellst ein **Fragewort** vor die Ja/Nein-Frage.

<u>Ja/Nein-Frage:</u>   *Is Susan from England?*
<u>Fragewortfrage:</u>   **Where** *is Susan from? England.*

<u>Ja/Nein-Frage:</u>   *Does Susan play hockey?*
<u>Fragewortfrage:</u>   **What** *does Susan play? Hockey.*

Kurzantworten

Auf Ja/Nein-Fragen kannst du **Kurzantworten** geben:
Yes, we do. / No, we don't.   *Yes, she does. / No, she doesn't.*
Yes, they are. / No, they aren't.   *Yes, he is. / No, he isn't.*

Questions – to do / to be

1. **Read the answers and write down the questions.**

    a) Q: sing / Jessica / does / in the choir?
       A: Yes, Jessica sings in the choir every Wednesday.
    b) Q: always / they / do / by bus / go?
       A: No, they usually go by bike.
    c) Q: from China / the new girl / is?
       A: No, she is from Vietnam.
    d) Q: football / Ryan / play / does?
       A: Yes, Ryan plays football on Tuesdays.
    e) Q: sometimes / do / you / in the park / meet?
       A: Yes, we often meet there after school.

2. **Complete the questions with "do / does" or "is / are".**

    a) _____ the children at Nottingham Junior School?
    b) _____ the boys in your team?
    c) _____ Isabelle her best friend?
    d) _____ the cat eat mice?
    e) _____ Mrs Grey the Maths teacher?
    f) _____ Lily and Grace sing in a band?

3. **Write down yes/no-questions in the simple present.**

    a) Cathy plays in the hockey team.
    b) The children eat pizza.
    c) The team meets after school.
    e) Betty and Carol play their favourite game on Wednesdays.
    f) The cat is white and black.

4. **Read the answers. Write down the questions with the correct question words.**

who	where	when	how	why	what

    a) … does Amelia live? – Amelia lives <u>in Sherwood</u>.
    b) … does Jake play? – Jake plays <u>the drums</u>.
    c) … feeds the cat? – <u>Anne's mum</u> feeds the cat.
    d) … do lessons finish? – Lessons finish <u>at 3.45 pm</u>.
    e) … does she usually get there? – She usually gets there <u>by train</u>.
    f) … are they late? – They are late <u>because the bus didn't come</u>.

5. **Write down yes/no-questions in the simple present.**

    a) we / get up / at 7 o'clock?
    b) your dad / prepare / our breakfast?
    c) the first lesson / start / at 9 o'clock?

Simple present

Questions – to do / to be

1. **Read the answers. Then write down the questions.**

    a) Q: play / Sue / does / hockey?
       A: Yes, Sue plays hockey every Wednesday.
    b) Q: always / they / do / by train / go?
       A: No, they usually go by bus.
    c) Q: from Germany / the new teacher / is?
       A: No, he is from Austria.
    d) Q: his friends / Kenny / meet / does?
       A: Yes, Kenny meets his friends on Tuesdays.

2. **Write down the questions. Use "do / does" oder "is / are". Write down short answers, too.**

    a) … the girls at Sherwood Junior School?   Yes, …
    b) … the boys in their room?   No, …
    c) … Cathy her sister?   Yes, …
    d) … the dog drink water?   Yes, …
    e) … Mrs Smith the English teacher?   No, …
    f) … Amy sing karaoke?   No, …
    g) … Betty and Jenny always do their homework?   Yes, …
    h) … the children meet in the shed at 8.00 am?   No, …
    i) … you sometimes drink Coke?   Yes, …

3. **Write down yes/no-questions in the simple present.**

    a) Emma plays in the school team.
    b) The children drink hot chocolate.
    c) The team meets in the break.
    e) Sam and David watch their favourite films on Wednesdays.
    f) The dog is brown and black.

4. **Write down yes/no-questions and complete the short answers.**

    a) Mrs Rose: …? – Susan: Yes, I usually do my homework alone.
    b) Mrs Rose: …? – Tom: No, we never ride our bikes to school.
    c) Mrs Rose: Does Jake play the drums in the school orchestra? – Susan: No, …
    d) Mrs Rose: And Jenny? Does she still play the flute? – Susan: Yes, ...
    e) Mrs Rose: …? – Derek: No, Mia doesn't play hockey.

5. **Ask about the underlined information. Write down questions with question words.**

who	where	when	how	what

    a) …? – <u>Chloe</u> usually feeds the cat.
    b) …? – The children meet <u>at 2 pm</u>.
    c) …? – Jake plays <u>the drums</u>.
    d) …? – They sing <u>at school</u>.
    e) …? – He usually feels <u>great</u> after a match.

Simple present

Statements – have got

Die Verwendung von „have got" im Simple Present

Mit „have got" kannst du im Simple Present ausdrücken, was jemand oder etwas **hat**.

Die Bildung des Simple Present von „have got"

Du bildest das Simple Present mit dem Infinitiv „have got". Bei der 3. Person Singular verkürzt sich der Verbstamm und du hängst ein **„s"** an.

I	have got	
you	have got	
he/she/it	ha**s** got	**Merksatz: "he, she, it – the ‚s' must fit"**
we	have got	
you	have got	
they	have got	

Kurzformen

Du kannst auch hier wieder **Kurzformen** verwenden:

I have got	→	I**'ve** got
you have got	→	you**'ve** got
he/she/it has got	→	he**'s**/she**'s**/it**'s** got
we have got	→	we**'ve** got
you have got	→	you**'ve** got
they have got	→	they**'ve** got

Simple present

Statements – have got

1. a. Tick the correct statements.
   b. Write down the wrong statements correctly.

   a) Sam have a new game. ☐
   b) Carol has got a rabbit. ☐
   c) The children has a great idea. ☐
   d) I have got blue trainers. ☐
   e) We have got an old car. ☐
   f) My family have a garden. ☐
   g) I has blonde hair. ☐
   h) Cathy and Susan have got the same skirt. ☐

2. Write down the sentences with "have got / has got".

   a) Emiliy … a cat.
   b) Mathew … two sisters.
   c) Betty … a brother.
   d) The Carters … a house.
   e) Jenny … a new computer.
   f) Jill … a red bike.

3. Write down sentences with the correct form of "have got".

   a) Lucy / sister.
   b) The Lincolns / new car.
   c) Tibby / basket.
   d) Jacob / guitar.
   e) London Junior High / library.
   f) The pupils / school uniform.

4. Write down sentences with "have got / has got".

The Evans	a garden
Dave	new bike
Ava	cat
Scarlett	red pencil case
Ben and Mia	their own rooms

5. Look at the pictures. Write down what they have got.

   a) 　　b) 　　c)

Simple present

Statements – have got

1. a. **Tick the correct statements.**
   b. **Write down the wrong statements correctly.**

   a) Grace have a new friend. ☐
   b) Emma has got a budgie. ☐
   c) The girls has a great idea. ☐
   d) I have got a pink skirt. ☐
   e) We have got an old house. ☐
   f) My family have got a new car. ☐
   g) I has got long hair. ☐
   h) David and Ben have got the same trainers. ☐

2. **Write down sentences with the correct form of "have got".**

   a) Eddie … a dog.
   b) Jane … two brothers.
   c) Becky … a sister.
   d) The Smiths … a flat.
   e) Jack … a new computer game.
   f) Carol … a yellow bike.
   g) Robert and Ben … a fan poster in their room.
   h) The family … a new car.
   i) Tibby … black jeans.
   j) Sam … a piano.
   k) London Junior High … a library.
   l) The pupils … a sandwich.

4. **Write down sentences with "have got / has got".**

The Browns	a house
Danny	new trainers
Noah and Ava	their own rooms
Charlotte	blue school bag
Kelly	hamster

5. **Look at the pictures. Write down what they have got.**

   a) 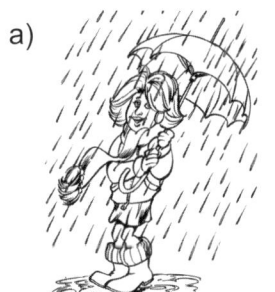   b)

6. **Write down the answers.**

   a) Has Lily got a sister? – No / Lily / a little brother
   b) Have the children got a green uniform? – No / the children / a grey uniform
   c) Have you got a new bike? – No / I / an old bike.

Simple present

Negation – have got

Die Verwendung von „have got" im Simple Present

Mit „have got" kannst du im Simple Present ausdrücken, was jemand oder etwas **hat** oder **nicht hat**.

Die Bildung der Verneinung mit „have got" im Simple Present

Du verneinst „have got" im Simple Present, indem du **„not"** zwischen „have/has" und „got" stellst.

I	have not got
you	have not got
he/she/it ha**s**	not got **Merksatz: "he, she, it – the ‚s' must fit"**
we	have not got
you	have not got
they	have not got

Kurzformen

Es ist üblich **Kurzformen** zu verwenden:

I have not got	→	I **haven't** got
you have not got	→	you **haven't** got
he/she/it has not got	→	he/she/it **hasn't** got
we have not got	→	we **haven't** got
you have not got	→	you **haven't** got
they have not got	→	they **haven't** got

Negation – have got

1. a. Tick the correct negative statements.
   b. Write down the wrong negative statements correctly.

   a) Jack has got not a new school bag. ☐
   b) Kate hasn't got a computer. ☐
   c) The children have not a great idea. ☐
   d) She haven't got blue trainers. ☐
   e) We haven't got a big garden. ☐
   f) My family hasn't got a car. ☐
   g) I have got not black hair. ☐
   h) Cathy and Isabelle haven't got the same pen. ☐

2. Complete the sentences with "haven't got / hasn't got".

   a) Lexie and Meredith … dog.
   b) David … a big brother.
   c) Linda … a pink skirt.
   d) The Whites … a flat.
   e) Margaret … a new computer.
   f) Carol … a red bike.

3. Write down negative statements.

   a) A bird has got long ears.
   b) My school has got three computer rooms.
   c) My sister has got a penfriend in Australia.
   d) I have got a little hamster.
   e) The pupils have got a pink school uniform.
   f) Sue and Sarah have got different dresses.

4. Write down the sentences with the negative form of "have got".

   a) Holly … a sister and a brother.
   b) The Millers … a new car.
   c) Sophie … a cup.
   d) Julia … a trumpet.
   e) Lincoln College … a library.
   f) The pupils … red shirts.

5. Write down what they haven't got.

a)	The Jones	a garden
b)	Benjamin	new bike
c)	Evie	cat
d)	Jessica	red pencil case
e)	Marc and Amy	their own rooms

Simple present

Negation – have got

1. a. Tick the correct negative statements.
   b. Write down the wrong negative statements correctly.

   a) Danny has got not an old school bag. ☐
   b) Maisie hasn't got a playstation. ☐
   c) The boys have not a great idea. ☐
   d) She haven't got a pink skirt. ☐
   e) We haven't got a big house. ☐
   f) My family hasn't got a flat. ☐
   g) I have got not new trainers. ☐
   h) Alex and Hannah haven't got the same jacket. ☐

2. Write down negative statements.

   a) A hamster has got long ears.
   b) My school has got a swimming pool.
   c) My brother has got a friend in China.
   d) I have got a little budgie.
   e) The children have got yellow school uniforms.
   f) Derek and Adam have got different trainers.

3. Write down negative statements.

   a) Ella and Freya … a dog.
   b) Dylan … a big brother.
   c) Katie … a pink shirt.
   d) The Whites … a flat.
   e) Isla … a new computer.
   f) Ryan … a red bike.

4. Write down what they haven't got.

a)	The Johnsons	a flat
b)	Luke	new bike
c)	Megan	hamster
d)	Samuel	green pencil case
e)	Dan and Ruby	their own rooms

5. Read the questions and write down the answers in complete sentences.

   a) Has Lucy got a hamster? – No, …
   b) Have the boys got a new ball? – No, …
   c) Have you got your own room? – No, …
   d) Have the girls got a green T-shirt? – No, …
   e) Has the school got a library? – No, …
   f) Has Cathy got a poster in her room? – No, …

Simple present

Questions – have got

Die Verwendung von „have got" im Simple Present

Mit „have got" kannst du im Simple Present ausdrücken und erfragen, was jemand oder etwas **hat** oder **nicht hat**.

Die Bildung von Fragen mit „have got" im Simple Present

Du kannst **2 Arten von Fragen** stellen und bilden:
1. Ja/Nein-Fragen (man kann nur mit ja oder nein antworten)
2. Fragen mit Fragewörtern

1. Ja/Nein-Fragen
   Du stellst das Subjekt zwischen „have" und „got".
   <u>Aussage</u>: *Susan* **has got** *a new skirt.*
   <u>Frage</u>: **Has** *Susan* **got** *a new skirt?*

2. Fragen mit Fragewort
   Du stellst ein Fragewort vor die Ja/Nein-Frage.
   <u>Ja/Nein-Frage</u>: *Has Susan got a new skirt?*
   <u>Fragewortfrage</u>: **What** *has Susan got? A new skirt.*

Kurzantworten

Wenn du eine Ja/Nein-Frage beantworten möchtest, reicht meist eine **Kurzantwort**.

Beispiel: *Has David got a sister?*   *Yes, he has. / No, he hasn't.*
          Have they got a car?   *Yes, they have. / No, they haven't.*

Simple present 29

Questions – have got

1. **Read the answers and write down the questions.**

   a) Q: a nice room / has / got / Carol?
      A: Yes, Carol has got a nice room.
   b) Q: a house / your family / has / got?
      A: No, my family hasn't got a house.
   c) Q: have / got / you / a TV in your room?
      A: No, I haven't got a TV in my room.
   d) Q: your school / has / a cafeteria / got?
      A: Yes, our school has got a cafeteria.
   e) Q: you / a cinema in your town / have / got?
      A: No, we haven't got a cinema in our town.

2. **Complete the questions with "have / has".**

   a) … the children got a nice teacher?
   b) … the boys got new trainers?
   c) … Becky got a computer?
   d) … the cat got a basket?
   e) … the school got a new gym?
   f) … Betty and Jenny got the same sneakers?

3. **Write down questions with "have got / has got".**

   a) you / a computer / in your room?
   b) your dad / a big car?
   c) you / your own room?
   d) Kate / a brother or a sister?

4. **Read the answers and complete the questions with the correct question words.**

who	where	when	why	what

   a) … has Susan got? – Susan has got <u>new shoes</u>.
   b) … has Sam got his CDs? – Sam has got his CDs <u>on a shelf</u>.
   c) … has got a brother? – <u>Cathy</u> has got a brother.
   d) … have your got time for me? – I have got time for you <u>at 3 o'clock</u>.
   e) … has she got an umbrella? – She has got an umbrella, <u>because there are black clouds</u>.

5. **Write down yes/no-questions with "have got / has got".**

   a) Chloe has got a big bed.
   b) The pupils have got a new teacher.
   c) The team has got blue shirts.
   d) Marc and Derek have got many friends.
   e) The rabbit has got a big cage.

Simple present

Questions – have got

1. **Read the answers and write down a matching question.**

   a) Q: a snack bar in your street / have / got / you?
   A: Yes, we've got a snack bar in our street.
   b) Q: a garden / your family / has / got?
   A: No, my family hasn't got a garden.
   c) Q: have / got / you / a computer in your room?
   A: No, I haven't got a computer in my room.
   d) Q: your school / has / a football ground / got?
   A: Yes, our school has got a football ground.

2. **Write down yes/no-questions with "have got".**

   a) the children / a modern school?
   b) the team / new coach?
   c) David / a computer?
   d) the dog / a basket?
   e) the school / a new playground?
   f) George and Mike / the same T-shirts?

3. **Write down yes/no-questions.**

   a) Cathy has got a small room.
   b) The children have got a new Maths teacher.
   c) The team has got green shorts.
   d) Tyler and Sam have got many friends.
   e) The budgie has got a big cage.

4. **Ask for the underlined information. Write down the questions with question words.**

who	where	when	why	what

   a) …? – Danny has got <u>new trainers</u>.
   b) …? – Sue has got her CDs <u>in a cupboard</u>.
   c) …? – <u>David</u> has got a sister.
   d) …? – I've got time for her <u>at 5 o'clock</u>.
   e) …? – She has got a raincoat, <u>because it is raining</u>.

5. **Write down yes/no-questions and complete the answers.**

   a) Mrs. Rose: …?
   Susan: Yes, we've got a big house for the family.
   b) Mrs. Rose: …?
   Tom: Yes, he has. Sam has got a hamster.
   c) Mrs. Rose: What about you Susan. Have you got a pet?
   Susan: Yes, …
   d) Mrs. Rose: Jenny, has your mum got her new car already?
   Jenny: No, … She … still … her old one.

Simple present

Statements

Die Verwendung des Going-to-future

Das Going-to-future ist eine Zeitform, die ausdrückt, was in der Zukunft geschehen wird.

Du verwendest sie immer dann,
- wenn du **Planungen** für die Zukunft ausdrücken möchtest.
  (Beispiel: *I am going to have a party on Saturday.*)
- du sagen möchtest, dass du eine **Vorahnung** hast oder du etwas kommen siehst.
  (Beispiel: *Look, the cars are going to crash!*)

Die Bildung des Going-to-future

Du bildest das Going-to-future folgendermaßen:

Form von *to be (am, are, is)* + *going to* + Verb im Infinitiv

Kurzform

Wie in vielen anderen Zeiten, kann man auch im Going-to-future die Kurzform in den Aussagesätzen verwenden:

1. I **am** going to buy a hamburger. → I**'m** going to buy a hamburger.
2. He **is** going to buy a hamburger. → He**'s** going to buy a hamburger.
3. They **are** going to buy a hamburger. → They**'re** going to buy a hamburger.

Signalwörter

Es gibt für das Going-to-future keine eindeutigen Signalwörter. Du musst erkennen, dass es um eine zukünftige Handlung geht und ob diese geplant oder vorhersehbar ist.
Dafür können die Signalwörter der Zukunft, wie: **tomorrow, next..., the following..., in 20XY**, hilfreich sein.

Statements

1. Translate into English and write down the correct sentences. Use the going-to future.

1. Pers. Sing.	Ich werde sitzen.
2. Pers. Sing.	Du wirst sitzen.
3. Pers. Sing.	Er wird sitzen.
1. Pers. Pl.	Wir werden sitzen.
2. Pers. Pl.	Ihr werdet sitzen.
3. Pers. Pl.	Sie werden sitzen.

2. Write down the following sentences in the correct order.

a) You / dance tonight / going to / are
b) I / going to / meet Sarah after school / am
c) My parents / going to / go on holiday next week / are
d) Going to / the boys / have a party at the weekend / are
e) The bus / is / arrive late this afternoon / going to
f) Are / Dan and Jim / going to / buy new tennis shoes on Saturday

3. Write down the following sentences in the going-to future.

a) She (meet) her best friend Tom.
b) They (do) their homework.
c) They (meet) in the cinema.
d) He (arrive) by bus at 10 o'clock.
e) I (watch) TV with you.
f) They (play) in the garden.

4. Translate the following sentences. Use the going-to future.

a) Am Wochenende werden wir unsere Großeltern besuchen.
b) Nächstes Jahr werden meine Eltern ein neues Auto kaufen,
c) Am Mittwoch werden wir unsere Hausaufgaben abends machen.
d) 2014 werde ich die Schule verlassen.
e) Mary wird sich heute Nachmittag neue Schuhe kaufen.
f) Jerry und Jim werden um 3 Uhr Fußball spielen.

5. Write down the short forms of the following sentences.

a) She is going to visit her father in the hospital.
b) We are going to have breakfast at 7 o'clock.
c) I am going to meet Sarah in the park.
d) He is going to call me after school.
e) She is going to play tennis with Marc.
f) You are going to be late tonight.

Going-to-future

Statements

1. **Translate the verbs and write down the correct English sentences in the going-to future.**

1. Pers. Sing.	haben
2. Pers. Sing.	gehen
3. Pers. Sing.	spielen
1. Pers. Pl.	tanzen
2. Pers. Pl.	anrufen
3. Pers. Pl.	laufen

2. **Write down correct sentences in the going-to future.**

   a) You / sleep late / tomorrow
   b) I / play tennis / in the evening
   c) My sisters / leave school / in the summer
   d) The dogs / play outside / in the afternoon
   e) The train / be late / this morning
   f) Carol and Sally / meet their friends / on Sunday

3. **Answer the following questions in the going-to future.**

   a) What is Sally going to do after school? – She / do / her homework / with Sam.
   b) What are the kids going to do after school? – They / play / in the garden.
   c) Where are the girls going to meet? – They / meet / in the restaurant.
   d) When is Peter going to come? – He / arrive / by train / in the evening.
   e) Who is going to play the guitar with me? – I / play / the guitar with you.
   f) Where are they going to go on holidays? – They / go / to Spain.

4. **Translate the following sentences and use – if possible – the short form of the going-to future.**

   a) Am Samstag werden wir die Müllers treffen.
   b) Nächstes Jahr wird meine beste Freundin nach London ziehen.
   c) Am Donnerstag werden sie sich einen Hund kaufen.
   d) 2013 werde ich heiraten.
   e) Megan wird heute Abend ins Kino gehen.
   f) Sie werden um fünf Uhr aufstehen.

5. **Write down the following sentences in the short form and underline the signal words of the going-to future.**

   a) He is going to visit his mother in the afternoon.
   b) They are going to meet in front of the cinema at 7 o'clock.
   c) You are going to write a good test tomorrow.
   d) She is going to meet me after school.
   e) Later, I am going to play football with my brother.
   f) Next Saturday, we are going to have lunch together.

Going-to-future

Negation

Die Verwendung des Going-to-future

Das Going-to-future ist eine Zeitform, die ausdrückt, was in der Zukunft (nicht) geschehen wird.

Du verwendest sie immer dann,
➢ wenn du Planungen für die Zukunft ausdrücken möchtest.
  (Beispiel: *I am not going to have a party on Saturday*.)
➢ du sagen möchtet, dass du eine Vorahnung hast, du etwas kommen siehst.
  (Beispiel: *Look, the cars aren't going to stop there!*).

Die Bildung der Verneinung im Going-to-future

Du bildest die Verneinung im Going-to-future, indem du „**not**" hinter das Hilfsverb stellst:

Form von *to be (am, are, is)* + *not* + *going to* + Verb im Infinitiv

Beispiel: *I am **not** going to take the train.*
  *He is **not** going to take the bus.*
  *We are **not** going to take the car.*

Kurzform

Bei der Verneinung verwendest du meist die **Kurzform**.

Beispiel: *I'm **not** going to take the train.*
  *He **isn't** going to take the bus.*
  *We **aren't** going to take the car.*

Going-to-future 35

Negation

1. **Look at the 8 sentences below. 5 are correctly negated.**
   a. **Mark the correct sentences with a tick (✓).**
   b. **Correct the wrong negations.**

   a) Mary is going to not open the window in the morning. ☐
   b) Sam and Carol aren't going to sleep in on Saturday. ☐
   c) My dog isn't going to go for a walk alone. ☐
   d) Sarah and her parents not are going to leave at 10 o'clock. ☐
   e) I'm not going to call you later this morning. ☐
   f) You aren't going to come to the party on Friday. ☐
   g) Larry is going to open not his present from Sue. ☐
   h) We aren't going to go on holiday this year. ☐

2. **Negate the following sentences correctly.**

   a) Michael is going to buy a new car on Friday.
   b) Mary and her best friend are going to go shopping after school.
   c) My grandparents are going to buy me a new bike next week.
   d) I'm going to do my homework at 2 o'clock.
   e) You're going to watch the new film tonight.
   f) Our teacher is going to leave school in summer.
   g) We're going to go on a class trip in June.

3. **Translate the following sentences.**

   a) Wir werden Sally nachmittags nicht treffen. (meet)
   b) Jim und Jack werden uns nicht bei den Hausaufgaben helfen. (help)
   c) Meine Eltern werden kein neues Haus kaufen. (buy)
   d) I'm not going to help you.
   e) We aren't going to travel to New York.
   f) She isn't going to cook dinner this evening.

4. **Write down the following sentences in the short form.**

   a) We are not going to write better tests next time.
   b) My brother is not going to ask the girl for her number.
   c) Our cats are not going to eat fish.
   d) Jeremy is not going to go to the cinema tonight.
   e) She is not going to answer the teacher's questions.
   f) You are not going to be the best in class this year.

4. **Write down the following sentences in the correct word order.**

   a) going – not – is – to – buy – she – tomatoes – lunch – for
   b) my – going – late – isn't – sister – come – to – late – home
   c) you – going – not – play – basketball – am – to – I – with

Going-to-future

Negation

1. **Write down correct negations in the going-to future. Translate the sentences into German.**

   a) Jeanny not is going to wash the dishes in the afternoon.
   b) Peter and Jim are going to not wash the car.
   c) Mum isn't not going to help me with my homework today.
   d) Dad and Uncle John not are going to come home in time.
   e) Peer and our dog not aren't going for a walk in the park this evening.
   f) I not am going to come to your party on Sunday.
   g) She is going to open not her present from Tommy.
   h) We going to go aren't to London this summer.

2. **Negate the following sentences correctly. Translate them into German.**

   a) Mum and dad are going to plan our trip to Jamaica.
   b) Tom is going to help me with my English vocabulary.
   c) My grandfather is going to visit us in June.
   d) I am going to meet Jenny in the park at 1 o'clock.
   e) You are going to buy new trousers in this shop.
   f) My new teacher is going to give us back our tests tomorrow.
   g) They are going to go to the museum at the weekend.

3. **Translate the following sentences into English and be careful to use the correct negation.**

   a) Ich werde dich nach der Schule nicht anrufen.
   b) Peter wird mir heute keine SMS schreiben.
   c) Unser Hund wird heute Abend nicht Gassi gehen.
   d) Sie werden uns am Wochenende nicht besuchen.
   e) Ich werde dich am Samstag nicht zur Party fahren.

4. **Look at the chart and write down correctly negated sentences in the going-to future. Take care with the word order.**

Who	When	What	Where/Who
Sarah	at 7 o'clock	get up	–
Jim and Ted	on Saturday	play tennis	outside
Mr Jones	at the weekend	wash the car	garage
My family	in the summer	drive	Spain
They	later	call	their friends
He	in the morning	go	to school

5. **Write down the following sentences in the short form.**

   a) We are not going to write better tests next time.
   b) My brother is not going to ask the girl for her number.
   c) Our cats are not going to eat fish.
   d) Jeremy is not going to go to the cinema tonight.
   e) She is not going to answer the teacher's questions.
   f) You are not going to be the best in class this year.

Going-to-future

Questions

Die Verwendung des Going-to-future

Das Going-to-future ist eine Zeitform, die ausdrückt, was in der Zukunft geschehen wird.

Du verwendest sie immer dann,
- wenn du **Planungen** für die Zukunft erfragen möchtest.
  (Beispiel: *Are you going to come to my party on Saturday?*)
- du sagen möchtest, dass du eine **Vorahnung** hast, du etwas kommen siehst.
  (Beispiel: *Look, are we going to crash into those cars?*)

Die Bildung der Frage im Going-to-future

Du bildest die Frage im Going-to-future folgendermaßen:

1. Möglichkeit

Form von *to be* (am, are, is) + Pers.pronomen + *going to* + Verb im Inf.

(Beispiel: *Are you going to come to my party?*
             Is he going to wash our car in the afternoon?)

2. Möglichkeit

Fragewort + Form von *to be* + Pers.pronomen + *going to* + Verb im Inf.

(Beispiel: *When are you going to come to my party?*
             Where is he going to wash our car?)

Going-to-future

Questions

1. **Read the following answers and write down the correct questions.**

    a) Q: you / going to / help / me / after school?
       A: Yes, I'm going to help you with your homework.

    b) Q: Tracy / going to / join / us on Wednesday?
       A: No, Tracy isn't going to join us. She's going to play tennis.

    c) Q: your mum / going to / work / tomorrow?
       A: Yes, my mum is going to work tomorrow in the afternoon.

    d) Q: you / going to / go / to the cinema / tonight?
       A: No, I'm not going to go to the cinema.

    e) Q: Sarah / going to / fly to France / in the summer?
       A: No, I think she's going to take the train to Italy.

2. **You ask your brother if he is going to do the following things. Write down your questions.**

    a) wash dad's car – on Friday

    b) have a party at home – next Saturday

    c) go on holiday with the family – in winter

    d) do your homework – in the afternoon

    e) watch TV with mum – at 8 o'clock

3. **Translate the following questions.**

    a) Wann werden wir uns heute Nachmittag treffen? (to meet / when)

    b) Wo wird Tom Tennis spielen? (to play / where)

    c) Wer wird uns begleiten? (to join / who)

    d) Warum werden deine Eltern ein neues Auto kaufen? (to buy / why)

    e) Wie wirst du mir helfen? (to help / how)

    f) Where is Sally going to wait for us?

    g) When are we going to get back our tests?

    h) Why isn't Jim going to play with us?

    i) Who is going to be in our team on Wednesday?

    j) Where are our parents going to eat in the evening?

Questions

1. **Read John's answers and write down the corresponding questions.**

   a) A: Yes, they're going to go to Spain in summer.

   b) A: No, Jim isn't going to come with his parents.

   c) A: Yes, his mum is going to work in Spain.

   d) A: No, I'm not going to visit the family there. I haven't got time.

   e) A: No, I think he isn't going to take the plane but the train.

   f) A: Yes, Jeremy and Jim are going to move to London in the summer.

   g) A: I don't know if Sally's mum is going to buy a dog for her birthday.

2. **You ask your best friend if he/she is going to do the following things.**
   a. Write down the correct questions.
   b. Your mum asks you about your friend's plans. What does she say?

a)	on Friday	come to Peter's party
b)	at the weekend	meet Sarah
c)	next summer	work in my dad's factory
d)	in the morning	take the bus to school
e)	after breakfast	go for a walk with my dog

3. **You ask your friend about his sister's plans for the weekend. Write down your questions.**

   a) Wird deine Schwester heute Nachmittag zu Hause sein?
   b) Werden ihre Freundinnen sie besuchen?
   c) Werden sie in den Park gehen?
   d) Wird sie am Samstag auch auf deiner Party sein?
   e) Werden ihre Freundinnen sie begleiten?

4. **Translate the following questions and take care with the question words you need.**

   a) Wann werden wir uns heute Nachmittag treffen?
   b) Wo wird Tom Tennis spielen?
   c) Wer wird uns begleiten?
   d) Warum werden deine Eltern ein neues Auto kaufen?
   e) Warum wirst du mir nicht helfen?
   f) Wie werdet ihr nach Frankreich fahren?
   g) Wann werden wir heute Abend essen?

Classroom

The classroom

Wenn du über dein Klassenzimmer sprechen möchtest, benötigst du Vokabeln zu dem Thema. Die wichtigsten findest du hier:

Things
Tafel – *blackboard*  Schwamm – *sponge*   Kreide – *chalk*
Tür – *door*   Fenster – *window*  Stuhl – *chair*
Schreibtisch – *desk* Tisch – *table*   Schrank – *cupboard*
Decke – *ceiling*   Regal – *shelf / shelves* (pl.) Landkarte – *map*
Poster – *poster*   Wand – *wall*   Fußboden – *floor*
Pinnwand – *pinboard*

Persons
Lehrer – *teacher*
Hausmeister – *caretaker*   Schüler – *pupil*
                            Schulleiter – *headmaster*

School stuff

Wenn du über Dinge in der Klasse sprechen möchtest, benötigst du die Vokabeln für bestimmte Arbeitsmaterialien und Schulsachen. Hier findest du die wichtigsten:

Füller – *pen*   Bleistift – *pencil*   Filzstift – *felt tip*
Radierer – *rubber*   Lineal – *ruler*   Buntstift – *coloured pencil*
Buch – *book*   Heft – *exercise book*   Notizblock – *note pad*
Klebestift – *glue stick* Schere – *scissors*   Tintenkiller – *ink eraser*

Mappe/Hefter – *folder*   Blatt Papier – *sheet of paper*
Arbeitsblatt – *worksheet*   Schultasche – *school bag*
Mäppchen – *pencil case*    Sporttasche – *sportsbag*
Wörterbuch – *dictionary*   Vokabelheft – *vocabulary book*

Verbs

Verben, die im Schulzusammenhang von Bedeutung sein können, sind diese:

arbeiten – *work*   schreiben – *write*   lesen – *read*
singen – *sing*   öffnen – *open*   schließen – *close*
zeichnen – *draw*   hinsetzen – *sit down*   aufstehen – *stand up*
umkreisen – *circle*   unterstreichen – *underline* still sein – *be quiet*
aufräumen – *tidy up*   herausholen – *take out* zuhören – *listen*
wegpacken – *put away*   (an)schauen – *look (at)* anhören – *listen to*

At school

Classroom

1. **Write down the correct English words.**

   a) alwl   c) ipcnel   e) lfroo
   b) batle   d) euglickst   f) dwoniw

2. **Write down the translation of the following words.**

   a) worksheet   c) cupboard
   b) pupil   d) folder

3. **Write down the following sentences and complete them.**

   a) This person is the boss of a school. It's the…
   b) You can clean the blackboard with it. It's the…
   c) You can put books on it. It's a…
   d) This person repairs things in your school. It's the…

4. **Look at the picture. Write down the English words for the things on the table. Begin the sentences with *"There is… / There are…"*.**

5. **Write down the translation of the verbs.**

   a) zeichnen   f) circle
   b) öffnen   g) underline
   c) lesen   h) close
   d) anhören   i) tidy up
   e) singen   j) be quiet

6. **Write down the following sentences and fill in the matching verbs.**

   | close | read | write | take out |

   a) Teacher: Let's start working. … your English books, please.
   b) Pupil: I'm cold. May I … the window, please?
   c) Teacher: Look at the short text on page 22. Who can … the text?
   d) Teacher: …your stories in your exercise books, please.

Classroom

1. **Put the letters in the correct order and write down the words.**

   a) helsf b) enplic c) edks d) alrcbbkoda

2. **Write down the German words.**

   a) chalk b) exercise book c) teacher d) ruler

3. **Who or what is it? Write down the English words. Start like this:** *"It's ..."*

   a) This person repairs things in a school.
   b) You can write with it on the blackboard.
   c) You can put your school stuff in it. You carry it on your back.
   d) You can put it on the wall. It has got a picture of the world on it.

4. **Describe the following things in your own words. Write down the English word for it.**

   a) Schwamm b) Mäppchen / Federtasche

5. **What can you see? Write down sentences. Start with** *"There is ... / There are ..."*.

6. **Write down the verbs in German.**

   a) draw d) circle
   b) open e) read
   c) put away f) sing

7. **Write down the following sentences. Fill in the matching verbs in English.**

   | öffnen | lesen | schreiben | herausholen | still sein | unterstreichen |

   a) Teacher: Let's start. … your Maths books, please.
   b) Pupil: It's hot. May I … the window, please?
   c) Teacher: Look at the words on page 31. Who can … the words?
   d) Teacher: … the words in your vocabulary books, please.
   e) Teacher: It's too loud. …, please.
   f) Teacher: Take a ruler and … the headline in green, please.

At school

Lessons

Lessons

Wenn du über den Unterricht in der Schule sprechen möchtest, benötigst du passende Vokabeln. Die wichtigsten sind hier aufgelistet:

Verbs

öffnen – *open*	schließen – *close*	schreiben – *write*
lesen – *read*	zeichnen – *draw*	unterstreichen – *underline*
umkreisen – *circle*	zuhören – *listen*	anhören – *listen to*
work – *arbeiten*	erklären – *explain*	buchstabieren – *spell*
erzählen – *tell*	wiederholen – *repeat*	(an)schauen – *look (at)*
still sein – *be quiet*	aufstehen – *stand up*	hinsetzen – *sit down*
fragen – *ask*	antworten – *answer*	abschreiben – *copy*

Things

Buch – *book*	Heft – *exercise book*	Mappe / Hefter – *folder*
Tafel – *blackboard*	Fenster – *window*	Tür – *door*

Classroom phrases – teacher

Diese Sätze kann dein Lehrer im Unterricht zu dir / deiner Klasse sagen:

Öffnet / Schließt bitte euer Buch.	*Open / Close your book(s), please.*
Arbeite bitte mit einem Partner.	*Work with a partner, please.*
Schreibe bitte in dein Heft.	*Write in your exercise book(s), please.*
Höre bitte gut zu.	*Listen carefully, please.*
Räume bitte deinen Arbeitsplatz auf.	*Tidy up your desk(s), please.*
Hole bitte deine Mappe heraus.	*Take out your folder(s), please.*
Buchstabiere das Wort bitte.	*Spell the word, please.*
Was bedeutet … auf Deutsch / Englisch?	*What is... in German / English?*
Wiederhole das bitte.	*Repeat, please.*
Schaue bitte das Bild an.	*Look at the picture, please.*

Classroom phrases – pupil

Diese Sätze kannst du zu deiner Klasse oder deinem Lehrer sagen:

Kannst du / Können Sie mir bitte helfen?	*Can you help me, please?*
Kann ich bitte … haben?	*Can I have a / an…, please?*
Hast du / Haben Sie bitte … für mich?	*Have you got a / an... for me, please?*
Kannst du / Können Sie bitte wiederholen?	*Can you repeat (it/that), please?*
Kannst du / Können Sie das bitte buchstabieren?	*Can you spell that, please?*
Darf ich bitte zur Toilette gehen?	*May I go to the toilet, please?*
I can see … in the picture.	*Ich sehe… auf dem Bild.*
Was bedeutet … auf Deutsch / Englisch?	*What is... in German / English?*
Ich habe das leider nicht verstanden.	*Sorry, I didn't understand.*

At school

Lessons

1. **Write down the correct English words.**

   a) letl
   b) labkcroabd
   c) wasnre
   d) olrefd
   e) ksa
   f) rdoo

2. **Write down the German meanings.**

   a) stand up
   b) repeat
   c) explain
   d) exercise book

4. **Look at the pictures. Match the sentences with the correct pictures.**

   A
   C
   B
   D

   a) May I go to the toilet, please?
   b) Listen carefully, please.
   c) Can you help me, please?
   d) Be quiet, please.

5. **Write down the dialogues and fill in the missing verbs.**

   | repeat | spell | copy | in German | I can see | exercise book |

   a) Pupil: Must we … the words from the blackboard?
      Teacher: Yes, write them in your …, please.
   b) Teacher: You need a hole punch for this.
      Pupil: What is 'hole punch' …?
   c) Teacher: Write down 'She opens her chest of drawers', please.
      Pupil: I can't write the word. Can you … 'chest of drawers', please?
   d) Teacher: What can you see?
      Pupil: … a red car in the picture.
   e) Pupil: What does '…' mean?
      Teacher: It means 'say it again'.

   At school

Lessons

1. **Write down the correct English words.**

   a) epsll c) rtewi e) stenli
   b) pretae d) ilfe f) iqtue

2. **Write down the German meanings.**

   a) ask c) look at e) circle
   b) answer d) tell f) draw

3. **Look at the pictures. Write down the German sentences in English and match them with the pictures.**

   A  C

   B 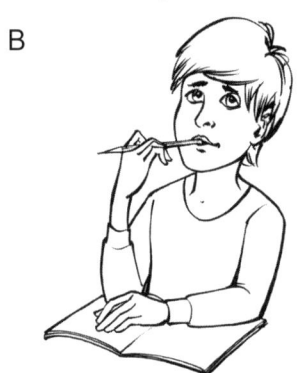 D

   a) Darf ich bitte auf die Toilette?
   b) Hört bitte gut zu!
   c) Können Sie mir bitte helfen?
   d) Seid bitte leise!

4. **Write down the dialogues and fill in the missing verbs in English.**

   | wiederholen | buchstabieren | abschreiben | auf Deutsch | Ich sehe | Heft |

   a) Pupil: Must we … the sentences in our grammar books?
      Teacher: No, not in your grammar books! Write them in your …, please.
   b) Teacher: You need a pencil sharpener for this.
      Pupil: What is 'pencil sharpener' …?
   c) Teacher: Write down 'she writes it into her diary', please.
      Pupil: I can't write the word. Can you … 'diary', please?
   d) Teacher: What can you see?
      Pupil: … a girl on a pony on the photo.
   e) Pupil: What does '…' mean?
      Teacher: It means 'say it again'.

At school

Numbers

Numbers from 0–100

Die Zahlen bis 100 findest du hier:

0 – zero	20 – twenty	30 – thirty
1 – one	21 – twenty-one	40 – **forty**
2 – two	22 – twenty-two	50 – **fifty**
3 – **three**	23 – twenty-three	60 – sixty
4 – four	24 – twenty-four	70 – seventy
5 – **five**	25 – twenty-five	80 – eighty
6 – six	26 – twenty-six	90 – ninety
7 – seven	27 – twenty-seven	
8 – eight	28 – twenty-eight	
9 – nine	29 – twenty-nine	100 – one hundred
10 – ten		
11 – eleven		
12 – twelve		
13 – **thirteen**	**Achtung:** Bei den markierten Zahlen musst du	
14 – fourteen	auf die richtige Schreibweise achten!	
15 – **fifteen**		
16 – sixteen		
17 – seventeen		
18 – eighteen		
19 – nineteen		

Numbers from 100–1000

Die Zahlen bis 1000 sind hier aufgelistet:

100 – one hundred	200 – two hundred
101 – one hundred and one	300 – three hundred
102 – one hundred and two	400 – four hundred
103 – one hundred and three	500 – five hundred
104 – one hundred and four	600 – six hundred
105 – one hundred and five	700 – seven hundred
106 – one hundred and six	800 – eight hundred
107 – one hundred and seven	900 – nine hundred
...	1000 – (one) a thousand

Talk about numbers and work with numbers

Wenn du über Zahlen redest und mit ihnen arbeitest, helfen dir diese Wörter:

zählen – *count*	rechnen – *calculate*	plus – *plus*
minus – *minus*	geteilt durch – *divided by*	mal – *times*
ist – *is / equals*	addieren – *add*	

At school

Numbers

1. **Find the numbers in the "word-snake" and write them down.**

   nosefivetreeelevendograbbtenmotherfiftyninecatsixhamstertwelve

2. **Write down the numbers in English (in words!).**

   a) hgeit
   b) ivfe
   c) wnetyt
   d) enelve
   e) noe
   f) tifenef

3. **Write down the numbers.**

   a) seventy-eight
   b) one hundred and ninety-five
   c) fourteen
   d) four hundred and ten
   e) fifty-two
   f) two

4. **Write down the numbers in English (in words!).**

   a) 12
   b) 18
   c) 30
   d) 56
   e) 109
   f) 354
   g) 45
   h) 99
   i) 13
   j) 0
   k) 1000
   l) 847

5. **What is the result? Calculate and write the result in English (in words!).**

   | 20 | 60 | 202 | 9 | 52 | 103 |

   a) 7 + 2 = …
   b) 25 – 5 = …
   c) 40 + 12 = …
   d) 10 · 6 = …
   e) 210 – 8 = …
   f) 99 + 4 = …

6. **What is the result?**
   a. **Match the exercises.**
   b. **Calculate and write down the result in English (in words!).**

   | 12 | 915 | 80 | 77 | 5 | 7 | 8 | 248 |

   a) ten – two = …
   b) two hundred and fifty four – six = …
   c) forty · two = …
   d) sixty-five + twelve = …
   e) nine hundred + fifteen = …
   f) one hundred and forty-four : twelve = …
   g) sixteen – eleven = …
   h) forty-nine : seven = …

   A) 16 – 11 = …
   B) 40 · 2 = …
   C) 49 : 7 = …
   D) 10 – 2 = …
   E) 900 – 15 = …
   F) 254 – 6 = …
   G) 144 : 12 = …
   H) 65 + 12 = …

   At school

Numbers

1. Find the words that match the topic in the "word-snake" and write them down.

2. Write down the numbers in English.

   a) sxiyt   c) inen   e) wot
   b) evnes   d) tentihre   f) ghtiye

3. Write down the correct numbers.

   a) ninety-six
   b) two hundred and sixty-nine
   c) fifteen
   d) one hundred and eleven
   e) sixty-two
   f) three

4. Write down the numbers in English (in words!).

   a) 13   c) 31   e) 239   g) 20   i) 1001
   b) 19   d) 0   f) 73   h) 52   j) 784

5. What is the right result?
   a. Write down the exercise in English first. For example: *two plus two is* …
   b. Then calculate and write down the result in English (in words!).

   | 19 | 40 | 303 | 11 | 54 | 102 |

   a) 9 + 2 = …
   b) 24 − 5 = …
   c) 43 + 11 = …
   d) 10 · 4 = …
   e) 310 − 7 = …
   f) 96 + 6 = …

6. What is the result? Calculate and write down the result in English (in words!).

   | 11 | 813 | 28 | 75 | 6 | 8 | 7 | 149 |

   a) ten minus three = …
   b) one hundred and fifty five minus six = …
   c) fourteen times two = …
   d) sixty-three plus twelve = …
   e) eight hundred plus thirteen = …
   f) one hundred and twenty-one divided by eleven = …
   g) sixteen minus ten = …
   h) forty-eight divided by six = …

At school

Time

Numbers from 1–60

Um über die Uhrzeit zu sprechen, benötigst du die Zahlen von 1 bis 60.

0 – zero	10 – ten	20 – twenty	30 – thirty
1 – one	11 – eleven	21 – twenty-one	40 – **forty**
2 – two	12 – twelve	22 – twenty-two	50 – **fifty**
3 – **three**	13 – **thirteen**	23 – twenty-three	60 – sixty
4 – four	14 – fourteen	24 – twenty-four	
5 – **five**	15 – **fifteen**	25 – twenty-five	
6 – six	16 – sixteen	26 – twenty-six	
7 – seven	17 – seventeen	27 – twenty-seven	
8 – eight	18 – eighteen	28 – twenty-eight	
9 – nine	19 – nineteen	29 – twenty-nine	

Achtung: Bei den markierten Zahlen musst du auf die richtige Schreibweise achten!

The time

So kannst du über die Uhrzeit sprechen:

It's three **o'clock**.

It's **half past** three. / It's three thirty.

It's **quarter past** three.
It's three fifteen.

It's **quarter to** four.
It's three forty-five.

Words and phrases

Wenn du über die Uhrzeit sprichst, benötigst du diese Redewendungen:

Uhr – *clock*	Armbanduhr – *watch*	Wecker – *alarm clock*
halb – *half*	vor – *to*	nach – *past*
viertel – *quarter*	Zeit – *time*	Es ist … – *It's …*
„punkt" – *o'clock*	um – *at*	Wann …? – *When…?*

Wie spät ist es? – *What time is it?*
Um wie viel Uhr …? – *At what time…?*

At school

Time

1. **Look at the clocks and write down the sentences with the matching words.**

half	past	o'clock	quarter	quarter	to	past

   a) It's two...

   b) It's ... two

   c) It's ... two.

   d) It's ... three.

2. **Match the clocks / watches and the correct times.**

   a) It's ten o'clock.
   b) It's quarter to six.
   c) It's quarter past twelve.
   d) It's half past seven.
   e) It's seven o'clock.
   f) It's quarter to three.
   g) It's half past four.
   h) It's quarter past two.

   A 07:00   B   C 04:30

   D   E   F 07:30

   G   H 05:45

3. **Write down the times in two different ways, e. g.:** *It's quarter past five. / It's five fifteen.*

   a) It's ....   b) It's ....   c) It's ....

   d) It's ....   e) It's ....   f) It's ....

4. **Write about David's day. Write down the following sentences and fill in the time in English.**

   a) David gets up at ...

   b) He eats his breakfast at ...

   c) David goes to school at ...

   d) The chess club starts at ...

   e) David comes home at ...

   f) He starts his homework at ...

   g) He meets his friends at ...

   h) He goes to bed at ...

   At school

Time

1. Match the clocks / watches and the correct times.

a) It's two o'clock.
b) It's quarter to four.
c) It's quarter past ten.
d) It's half past nine.
e) It's five o'clock.
f) It's quarter to eight.
g) It's half past three.
h) It's quarter past one.

A
B
C
D 03:30
E
F 09:30
G
H 03:45

2. Write down the times in two different ways, e. g.: *It's quarter past five. / It's five fifteen.*

a) It's ….
b) It's ….
c) It's ….
d) It's ….
e) It's ….
f) It's ….

3. Write about Sam's day. Write down the sentences and fill in the right times in English.

a) Sam gets up at …
b) He eats his breakfast at …  07:50
c) Sam goes to school at ….
d) The computer club starts at … 15:30
e) Sam comes home at …
f) He starts his homework at …. 17:40
g) He meets his friends at ….
h) He goes to bed at …. 20:45

4. Write about Susan's day. Write down correct English sentences.

a) (get up)
b) (have breakfast) 07:45
c) (feed the cat)
d) (go to school) 08:15
e) (come home)
f) (do her homework) 16:45
g) (meet friends)
h) (go to bed) 20:45

At school

Timetable

Subjects (Fächer)

Damit du deine Unterrichtsfächer benennen kannst, ist hier eine Liste:

Languages (Sprachen)
Deutsch – *German*   Englisch – *English*   Latein – *Latin*
Französisch – *French*   Spanisch – *Spanish*   Türkisch – *Turkish*

Science (Naturwissenschaft)
Biologie – *biology*   Chemie – *chemistry*   Physik – *physics*

Others (Andere)
Geschichte – *history*   Kunst – *arts*
Gemeinschaftskunde – *social studies*   Theater AG – *drama group*
Erdkunde – *geography*   Chor – *choir*
Religion – *RE (religious education/instruction)*   Orchester – *orchestra*
Sport – *PE (physical education)*   Schulband – *school band*
Arbeitslehre – *CDE (craft/design/technology)*   Projekt – *project*
IT/Computerkurs – *computer technology*   Klassenstunde – *tutor lesson*

Things you learn about – Nouns

Mit diesen Vokabeln kannst du über die Unterrichtsfächer sprechen:

Zahlen – *numbers*   Instrument – *instrument*   PC – *computer*
Menschen – *people*   Völker – *peoples/nations*   Stadt – *city*
Fluss – *river*   Berg – *mountain*   Land – *country*
Welt – *world*   Klima – *climate*   Tier – *animal*
Pflanzen – *plants*   Körper – *body*   Gott – *God*
Theaterstück – *play*   Präsentation – *presentation*   Glaube – *belief*
Sportarten – *sports*   Probleme – *problems*   Holz – *wood*
Metall – *metal*   Küche – *kitchen*   Essen – *food*

Adjectives and Verbs

Diese Verben und Adjektive helfen dir, über Unterrichtsfächer zu sprechen:

einfach – *easy*   schwierig – *difficult*
interessant – *interesting*   langweilig – *boring*
gut sein in – *be good at*   Lieblings ... – *favourite*
schlecht sein in – *be bad at*

spielen – *play*   zeichnen – *draw*
(an)hören – *listen (to)*   arbeiten (mit) – *work (with)*
machen/tun – *do*   arbeiten (an) – *work (on/at)*
lernen (von/über) – *learn (about)*   sprechen (über/mit) – *talk (about/with)*
diskutieren – *discuss*

At school

Timetable

1. Write down the words that match the topic in the "word-snake".

easymothertimetablebathroomsubjectswimmingpoolscienceparentsarts

2. Write down the subjects in English.

   a) mreang
   b) mictshrye
   c) hcrio
   d) ehcnotogyl

3. Write down the German translation of the following words.

   a) peoples
   b) belief
   c) wood
   d) a play
   e) drama group
   f) body

4. Write down the sentences and fill in the missing words in English.

hsiroty   chtkine   oregpgahy   lpntas   nimasla   obdy   glaugnesa   chnetolygo

   a) You learn about the world, countries, mountains and rivers in …
   b) In … you work with wood or you do cooking in the …
   c) In Biology you learn about …, … and your …
   d) Spanish, French, Turkish and English are different …
   e) In … you talk about old times and different peoples or old kings and queens.

5. Write down the adjectives and verbs in English or in German.

   a) boring
   b) work with
   c) learn about
   d) easy
   e) interessant
   f) Lieblings…
   g) schwierig
   h) spielen

6. Write down the reports and fill in the missing words.

   | climate   favourite   draw   mountains   maths   arts |
languages   PE   geography   French   rivers   sports

   a) David's … subject is… He likes numbers and he is very good at it.
      He likes…, too. David likes football, basketball and other different…
   b) Cathy likes… She is good at painting and she likes colours.
      She can… with a pencil, chalk or watercolours.
   c) Betty and Susan like all… They love learning vocabulary and grammar.
      They like… best, because they like crepes and baguettes.
   d) Robert is good at… He knows a lot about… like the Danube or about
      … like the Alps. He likes talking about the weather or the… in other countries.

At school

Timetable

1. **Write down the subjects in English.**

    a) thmsa
    b) shiroty
    c) mdara upog
    d) cesince

2. **Write down the German translation of the following words.**

    a) choir
    b) school orchestra
    c) geography
    d) craft/design/technology
    e) animals

3. **Write down the following sentences and fill in the missing words in English.**

Holz Biologie Französisch Kochen Länder Englisch Körper Pflanzen Berge

    a) You learn about the world, ..., ... and rivers in geography.
    b) In technology you work with ... or you do ... in the kitchen.
    c) In ... you learn about ..., animals and your ...
    d) Spanish, ..., Turkish and ... are different languages.

4. **Explain the words in English. Write sentences in your own words.**

    a) IT
    b) Schulband

5. **Write down the adjectives and verbs in English.**

    a) langweilig
    b) listen to
    c) lernen über
    d) difficult
    e) interesting
    f) Lieblings…
    g) leicht
    h) play / act

6. **Write down the reports and fill in the missing words in English.**

Klima Sport zeichnen Mathe Kunst Sprachen
Lieblings Erdkunde Spanisch Flüsse Sportarten

    a) Sam's ... subject is... He likes numbers and he is very good at it.
       He likes…, too. Sam likes tennis, hockey and other different…
    b) Susan likes… She is good at painting and she likes colours.
       She can… with coloured pencils, chalk or watercolours.
    c) Kate and Sue like all… They love learning vocabulary and grammar.
       They like … best, because they like tortillas and tapas.
    d) Danny is good at… He knows a lot about … like the Thames or about
       mountains like the Alps. He likes talking about the weather or the … in other countries.

At school

Prepositions

Prepositions

Mit Präpositionen kannst du genaue Angaben machen, wo sich Personen oder Dinge befinden.
Die wichtigsten findest du hier:

unter – *under*	*The pen is under the table.*
auf – *on*	*The rubber is on the chair.*
auf – *onto*	*He's stepping onto the stage.*
an – *on/at*	*There is a note on the pinboard.*
in/im – *in*	*The bag is in the cupboard.*
in (hinein) – *into*	*I put my book into my school bag.*
neben – *next to*	*He is sitting next to Mike.*
zwischen – *between*	*She is sitting between Sue and Cathy.*
hinter – *behind*	*The girl is behind the table.*
vor – *in front of*	*The teacher is in front of the blackboard.*
über – *over*	*There is a poster over the shelf.*
über – *above*	*The lamps are above our heads.*
gegenüber – *opposite*	*The window is opposite the door.*
innen – *inside*	*Let's play inside.*
außen – *outside*	*Don't go outside, it's cold.*

Phrases

Diese Ausdrücke helfen dir, über die Position von Personen und Dingen zu sprechen:

Wo ist ...? – *Where is...?*
Wo sind ...? – *Where are...?*
Es gibt ... / Da ist.... – *There is...*
Es gibt ... / Da sind...– *There are...*
Es ist ... – *It is...*
Sie sind ... – *They are...*

56 At school

Prepositions

1. Write down the prepositions in English.

   a) hndibe   c) popoiste   e) ot extn
   b) dsiine   d) webente   f) drenu

2. Write down the following sentences. Fill in *"There is … / There are …"*.

   a) … five felt tips on my desk.
   c) … a schoolbag under the table.
   b) … a poster next to the pinboard.
   d) … pupils in the classroom.

3. Write down the questions and fill in *"Where is … / Where are …"*.

   a) … my new CDs?
   b) … Sarah's exercise book?
   c) … the English books?
   d) … your exercise book?

4. Match the sentences with the pictures.

   a)    c)

   b)    d)

   A The cat is behind the sofa.
   B The cat is under the sofa.
   C The cat is next to the sofa.
   D The cat is on the sofa.

5. Write down the sentences and fill in the missing prepositions.

between	under	in front of	next to	behind	on	in

   a) The chair is … the desk. (hinter)
   b) The pencil case is … the table. (unter)
   c) The teacher is … of the board. (vor)
   d) One boy is sitting … a girl. (neben)
   e) There are two boys sitting … the boy and the girl. (zwischen)
   f) The book is … the desk. (auf)
   g) The ruler is … the schoolbag. (in)

At school

Prepositions

1. **Write down the prepositions in English.**

    a) auf / an   c) gegenüber   e) neben
    b) in   d) zwischen   f) unter

2. **Write down sentences in English. Use *"There is … / There are …"*.**

    a) 5 Buntstifte / auf meinem Schreibtisch.
    c) ein Mäppchen / unter dem Schrank.
    b) eine Landkarte / neben der Pinwand.
    d) Schüler / im Klassenzimmer.

3. **Write down the questions in English. Use *"Where is … / Where are …"*.**

    a) …?
       Your books are on your bed.
    b) …?
       Betty's ruler is in Sam's school bag.
    c) …?
       The dictionaries are in the shelf.
    d) …?
       Your pencil case is on your desk.

4. **Look at the pictures. Write down suitable sentences in English.**

    a)

    c)

    b)

    d)

5. **Write down the sentences and fill in the prepositions in English.**

    a) The girl is … the desk. (hinter)
    b) The pen is … the table. (unter)
    c) The teacher is … of the board. (vor)
    d) One boy is sitting … a girl. (neben)
    e) There are two girls sitting … two boys. (zwischen)
    f) The pencil case is … the desk. (auf)
    g) The book is … the schoolbag. (in)

At school

Family members

Family members

Wenn du über deine Familie sprechen möchtest, benötigst du einige wesentliche Vokabeln. Die wichtigsten findest du hier:

Vater / Papa	*father / dad*	Ehemann	*husband*
Mutter / Mama	*mother / mum*	Ehefrau	*wife*
Eltern	*parents*	Kinder	*children*
Bruder	*brother*	Sohn	*son*
Schwester	*sister*	Tochter	*daughter*
Großmutter / Oma	*grandmother / grandma*	Enkelin	*granddaughter*
Großvater / Opa	*grandfather / grandpa*	Enkel	*grandson*
Urgroßeltern	*great-grandparents*	Urenkel	*great-grandson*
Onkel	*uncle*	Patenonkel	*godfather*
Tante	*aunt*	Patentante	*godmother*
Nichte	*niece*	Patenkind	*godchild*
Neffe	*nephew*	Braut	*bride*
Cousin	*cousin*	Bräutigam	*groom*
Cousine	*cousin*	Zwilling	*twin*

Verbs

Verben, die in diesem Zusammenhang von Bedeutung sein können, findest du hier:

wohnen	*to live*	mögen	*to like*
kommen (aus)	*to come from*	lieben	*to love*
zusammenleben	*to live together*	nicht mögen	*to dislike*
umziehen	*to move*	hassen	*to hate*
		sich verlieben	*to fall in love*
heiraten	*to marry*		
sich scheiden lassen	*to get divorced*	anrufen	*to call*
streiten	*to quarrel with sb.*	abholen	*to catch*
bekommen	*to get*	besuchen	*to visit*
erziehen	*to bring up*	treffen	*to meet*
adoptieren	*to adopt*	schreiben	*to write*
schwanger sein	*to be pregnant*	sehen	*to see*
taufen	*to baptize*		
sterben	*to die*		
gebären	*to give birth*		
verlobt sein	*to be engaged*		

At home

Family members

1. Write down the following words in English.

a) Mutter

b) Großvater

c) Neffe

d) Tante

e) Patenonkel

f) Schwester

g) Sohn

2. Which persons are described in the following sentences? Fill in.

brother	grandparents	grandmother	niece	parents	aunt

a) She is my grandfather's wife, so she is my ...

b) He is my parents' son, so he is my ...

c) She is my brother's daughter, so she is my ...

d) They are my mother's parents, so they are my ...

e) She is my mother's sister, so she is my ...

f) My mother and father are my ...

3. Translate the following verbs into German

a) to get divorced

b) to like

c) to bring up

d) to die

e) to meet

4. Translate the following sentences into English.

a) Wir besuchen meine Großeltern.

b) Ich mag meine Schwester und meinen Bruder.

c) Sie mag ihren Cousin nicht.

d) Meine Schwester heiratet meinen Freund.

At home

Family members

1. Look at the sentences below.
   a. Fill in the missing German words.
   b. Translate the sentences into English.

   a) Mein ... ist der Mann meiner Mutter.
   b) Großvaters Frau ist meine ...
   c) Die Schwester meines Neffen ist meine ...
   d) Mein ... ist der Bruder meiner Mutter.
   e) Meine ... ist die Tochter meiner Mutter.
   f) Die ... meines Vaters ist meine Schwester.
   g) Die Brüder meiner Nichte sind meine ...

2. Which people are described in the following sentences?
   a. Fill in the missing words.
   b. Translate the sentences into German

   a) He's my aunt's husband. So, he's my...
   b) She's my sister, so she's my father's...
   c) They're my brother's mother and father, so they're my ..., too.
   d) She's my mother's mother, so she's my...
   e) He's my uncle's son, so he's my...
   f) She's my aunt's daughter, so she's my mother's...

3. What do you call the person of the opposite sex?
   a) mother
   b) uncle
   c) niece
   d) husband
   e) granddaughter
   f) brother
   g) cousin

4. Fill in the missing words and complete the sentences correcty.
   a) My parents are divorced. That's why they don't … anymore.
   b) I like my brother very much. I really … him.
   c) I'm very sad because my grandmother will … soon. She's 90 years old.
   d) In summer I'll get a brother or sister. My mum is…
   e) I must leave my old school because we're going to … to Berlin.

5. Translate the following sentences into English.
   a) Ich mag meinen Bruder.
   b) Meine Eltern lieben meine Schwester und mich.
   c) Er hasst seine Cousine.
   d) Wir besuchen unsere Großeltern.
   e) Meine Tante und mein Onkel heiraten.
   f) Mein Bruder und ich sind Zwillinge.
   g) Die Braut und der Bräutigam leben zusammen in London.

Our house

The house

Wenn du über dein Zuhause sprechen möchtest, benötigst du einige wesentliche Vokabeln. Die wichtigsten findest du hier:

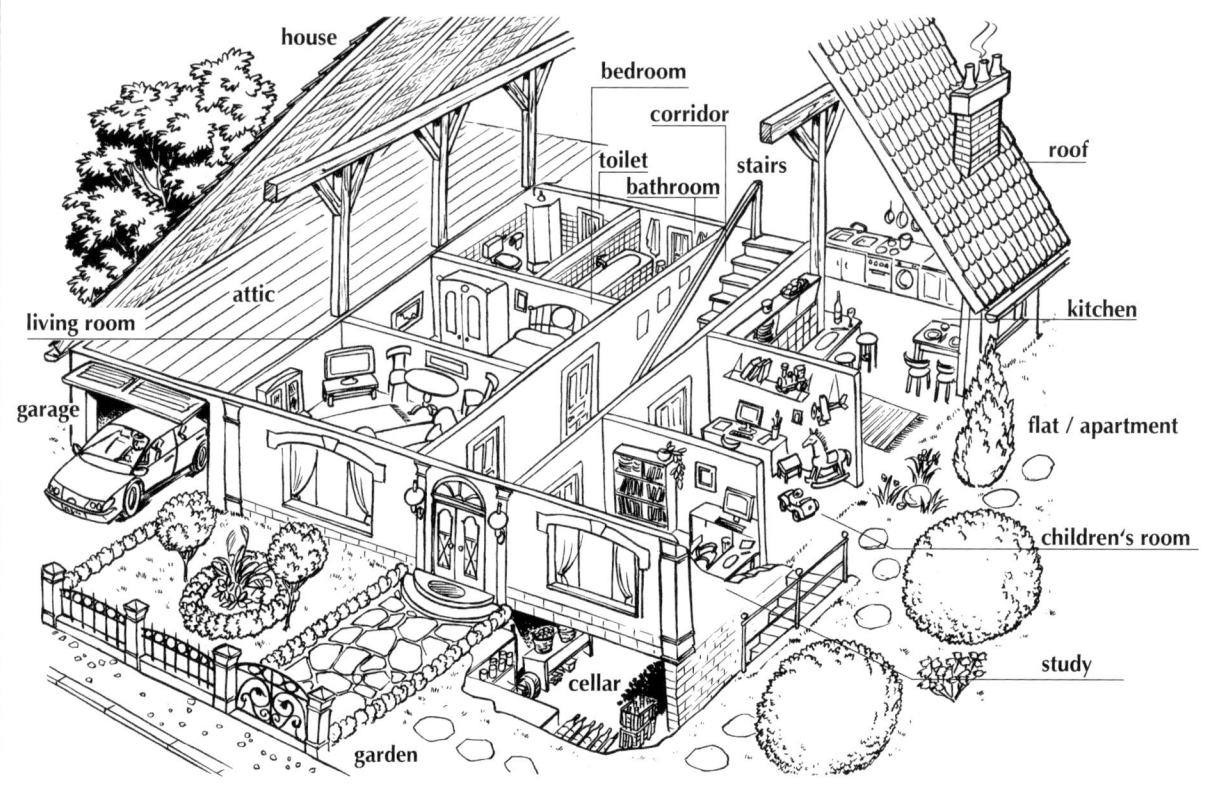

Furniture

Wenn du Räume beschreiben möchtest, benötigst du die Vokabeln für bestimmte Möbelstücke und weiteres Inventar. Hier findest du die wichtigsten:

Schrank	cupboard	Bett	bed	Spülmaschine	dishwasher
Tisch	table	Trockner	drier	Waschbecken	washbasin
Stuhl	chair	Schreibtisch	desk	Waschmaschine	washing machine
Backofen	oven	Sofa	sofa/couch	Dusche	shower
Herd	cooker/stove	Regal	shelf	Toilette	toilet
Spüle	(kitchen) sink	Garderobe	wardrobe	Badewanne	(bath) tub

Verbs

Verben, die in diesem Zusammenhang von Bedeutung sein können, findest du hier:

wohnen	to live	arbeiten	to work	schlafen	to sleep
kaufen	to buy	bauen	to build	baden	to take a bath
mieten	to rent	putzen	to clean	duschen	to take a shower
fernsehen	to watch TV	aufräumen	to tidy up	waschen	to wash
spielen	to play	kochen	to cook		

At home

Our house

1. Translate the following rooms into English.

   a) Küche
   b) Arbeitszimmer
   c) Bad
   d) Wohnzimmer
   e) Keller

2. Which rooms are described by the following sentences? Start your sentences like this: *This room is...*

kitchen   children's room   study

   a) It's the room where you find a desk, a chair and often some shelves.
   b) It's the room where you normally prepare food or come together to eat.
   c) It's the room where you sleep at night and where all your toys are in.

3. Write down sentences about the following rooms and the furniture inside. Start with: *In the... there is / there are...*

a)	kitchen	dishwasher
b)	garage	cars, bikes
c)	bedroom	bed, wardrobe
d)	bathroom	shower, toilet
e)	study	desk, chair, shelves

4. Write down the translation of the following verbs.

   a) work
   b) sleep
   c) play
   d) tidy up

   e) rent
   f) buy
   g) take a shower
   h) wash

5. Complete the following sentences with one of the verbs below.

take   live   tidy up   play   sleep   build

   a) We ... in a house near our school. It's a big house with a red roof.
   b) My parents ... a new house at the end of the street.
   c) I hate to ... my room. My mum always says that my toys are in her way.
   d) I love to ... on the computer in my dad's study. I have got many computer games.
   e) In the morning, I always ... a shower.
   f) My sister and I ... in one room. But we don't have only one bed of course!

At home

Our house

1. **Translate the following sentences into English.**

    a) Unsere Küche ist sehr groß.
    b) Mein Vater hat ein neues Arbeitszimmer.
    c) Das Bad ist grün.
    d) Der Fernseher ist im Wohnzimmer.
    e) Wir haben einen kleinen Keller.

2. **Write correct sentences about the following rooms and use the words given below. Start like this:** *The... is the room where...*

    a) living room – room, watch TV, family comes together, the evening
    b) bathroom – room, take a shower, in the morning, sometimes take a bath
    c) bedroom – room, your parents sleep, at night, you often find a bed, a wardrobe

3. **Look at the list below.**
    a. Write down in which room you can find these things.
    b. Write down sentences about the rooms and the things inside. Start like this:
       In the... you can find...

a)	dishwasher
b)	car, bikes
c)	bed, wardrobe
d)	shower, toilet
e)	desk, chair, shelves

4. **What is the English translation for the following verbs? Write down the words in English.**

    a) schlafen
    b) spielen
    c) saubermachen
    d) arbeiten
    e) kaufen
    f) mieten
    g) waschen
    h) aufräumen

5. **Complete the following sentences. Fill in the missing words.**

    a) We don't ... in a big house but in a small flat.
    b) My parents ... our clothes in the washing machine in the cellar.
    c) We don't like to ... our rooms. There are always so many toys on the floor.
    d) My parents don't go to an office. They ... at home in their study.
    e) Every Saturday, my sister and I have to ... in our bathroom. We always sit in the tub together.
    f) Today, we are going to ... a new house with a big garden. It costs a lot of money.
    g) I can't ... very well because our hamster is very noisy at night.

Sports and hobbies

Sports

Wenn du über Sportarten sprechen möchtest, benötigst du einige wesentliche Vokabeln. Die wichtigsten findest du hier:

Fußball	*football*		Inlineskaten	*(inline) skating*
Handball	*handball*		Basketball	*basketball*
Volleyball	*volleyball*		Tennis	*tennis*
Schwimmen	*swimming*		Tischtennis	*table tennis*
Reiten	*riding*		Segeln	*sailing*
Fahrrad fahren	*biking*		Surfen	*surfing*
Leichtathletik	*athletics*		Schlittschuh	*ice skating*
Squash	*squash*		Baseball	*baseball*
Golf	*golf*		Kanufahren	*canoeing*
Klettern	*rock climbing*		Tauchen	*diving*

Bezeichnungen für Orte, an denen man Sport treiben kann:

Sportplatz	*sports field*	Platz (Tennis, Squash ...)	*court*
Turnhalle	*gym*	Stadion	*stadium*
Golfplatz	*golf course*	Weg/Pfad	*track*
Schwimmbad	*swimming pool*		

Bezeichnungen für Menschen, die mit Sport zu tun haben:

Athlet	*athlete*	Trainer	*trainer*
Fan	*fan*	Veranstalter	*organizer*
Zuschauer	*spectator*	Spieler	*player*
Reporter	*reporter*	Mannschaft	*team*

Hobbies

Wenn du über deine Hobbys sprechen möchtest, benötigst du einige wesentliche Verben, die Freizeittätigkeiten beschreiben:

lesen	*to read*		laufen	*to run/to jog*
schreiben	*to write*		treffen	*to meet*
Musik hören	*to listen to music*		singen	*to sing*
fernsehen	*to watch TV*		telefonieren	*to call*
spielen	*to play*		machen	*to do*
tanzen	*to dance*		schwimmen	*to swim*
Fahrrad fahren	*to ride a bike*		reiten	*to ride a horse*
skaten	*to skate*		surfen	*to surf*

Verwendest du die Verben als Subjekt, musst du ein *-ing* anhängen!

At home

Sports and hobbies

1. **What are the English words for the following sports?**

   a) Surfen

   b) Tauchen

   c) Leichtathletik

   d) Golf

   e) Handball

   f) Tischtennis

   g) Fußball

   h) Volleyball

2. **Translate the German words and write down complete English sentences.**

   a) My favourite sport is… (*Fußball*).

   b) I also like … very much (*Klettern*).

   c) My mum and dad like … the best (*Segeln*).

   d) My sister is very good at… (*Tischtennis*).

   e) My big brother is a real … fan (*Surfen*).

   f) I really want to try… (*Reiten*). But I don't like horses very much.

3. **Fill in the places where the following sports take place and write down complete sentences.**

   a) You play tennis on a...   1) stadium

   b) People go jogging on a...   2) gym

   c) You play handball in a...   3) court

   d) Big football teams play in a... 4) track

4. **Look at the words below.**
   a. Write down the English expressions for the following German words.
   b. Which two words are exactly the same in English?

   a) Athlet   d) Trainer

   b) Reporter   e) Spieler

   c) Veranstalter   f) Mannschaft

Sports and hobbies

1. **Peter loves doing sports. Write sentences about which sports he likes. Start with:** *Peter likes...*

   a) Schwimmen
   b) Reiten
   c) Fahrrad fahren
   d) Leichtathletik
   e) Fußball
   f) Tischtennis
   g) Klettern
   h) Kanufahren

2. **Translate the following sentences into English.**

   a) Mein Lieblingssport ist Volleyball.
   b) Ich hasse Tauchen.
   c) Meine Eltern mögen Schlittschuh laufen.
   d) Meine Schwester ist sehr gut im Tanzen.
   e) Mein kleiner Bruder ist ein Handballfan.
   f) Mein Freund Tony spielt Golf.

3. **Which places for doing sports are meant? Write down the sentences mentioning the correct places.**

   a) You play tennis there if the weather is nice.
   b) Normally people go jogging in the forest on it.
   c) You play volleyball or handball there.
   d) People do athletics there. It's very big.

4. **What's the expression for the following persons? Complete the sentences.**

   a) A person who comes to every game of his favourite team is a really big...
   b) Every team needs a ... to become better.
   c) When you watch a football game on TV, there are always ... who speak about the match.

5. **Look at the chart and write down correct English sentences about what the people like to do.**

Sarah	Bücher lesen
Tom	Tischtennis spielen
Jamie	Lieder schreiben
Mary	Freunde anrufen
die Mädchen	im Park joggen gehen
Mama und Papa	Musik hören
unser Hund	im Garten herumrennen
wir	Tanzen

At home

Animals and pets

Animals

Wenn du über Tiere sprechen möchtest, benötigst du einige wesentliche Vokabeln. Die wichtigsten findest du hier:

Schwein	*pig*		
Zebra	*zebra*		
Ente	*duck*	 *crocodile*	*snail*  *cow*
Huhn	*chicken*	 *tiger*	*horse*  *sheep*
Löwe	*lion*		
Bär	*bear*		
Schlange	*snake*		
Affe	*monkey*		
Eisbär	*polar bear*	 *elephant*	*butterfly*  *donkey*
Wal	*whale*		
Hai	*shark*		

Stall / Scheune	*barn*	Hasenstall	*hutch*
Hühnerstall	*hen house*	Pferdestall	*stable*

Pets

Wenn du über Haustiere sprechen möchtest, benötigst du einige wesentliche Vokabeln. Die wichtigsten findest du hier.

 *cat*  *dog*  *rabbit*  *goldfish*  *parrot*

Maus	*mouse*	Meerschweinchen	*guinea pig*
Hamster	*hamster*	Schildkröte	*turtle*
Wellensittich	*budgie*		
Käfig	*cage*	Hundehütte	*kennel*
Aquarium	*aquarium*	Terrarium	*terrarium*

Verbs

Verben, die in diesem Zusammenhang von Bedeutung sein können:

laufen	*to run*	klettern	*to climb*
springen / hüpfen	*to jump*	schwimmen	*to swim*
bellen	*to bark*	spielen	*to play*
singen	*to sing*	riechen	*to smell*
fliegen	*to fly*	beißen	*to bite*
jagen	*to hunt*	kriechen	*to crawl*
füttern	*to feed*	säubern	*to clean*

At home

Animals and pets

1. What's the English name of the following animals?

   a)  b) 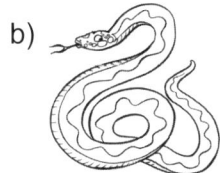 c)  d)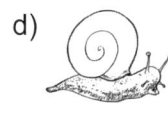

   e)  f)  g)

2. Which animals are meant here? Start with: *It's ...*

horse	snake	cow	lion

   a) This animal lives on a farm and eats grass. We get our milk from it

   b) This animal can run quickly and jump high. You can ride on it.

   c) Some people are afraid of this animal. It is very quiet and crawls on the floor.

   d) These animals live in Africa and can run quickly. They hunt and eat other animals.

3. There are 6 mistakes in the information about the elephant. Underline them and then correct the text.

   Elephants are big insects. They are green. They eat other animals. They can fly. Elepahnts live in the forests of Europe. Some people hunt elephants because of their trunks.

4. What do the following verbs mean in German? Write them down.

   a) jump
   b) fly
   c) feed
   d) swim

   e) smell
   f) clean
   g) play
   h) bark

5. Write down complete sentences about the following animals.

   a) tiger – hunt – other animals – jungle
   b) polar bear – live – north pole
   c) monkey – jump – tree to tree
   d) cat – lie – in front of – stove

At home

Animals and pets

1. **Translate the following sentences about animals into German.**

   a) The lion lives in Africa and has got a long brown mane.
   b) A snake crawls on the floor and many people are afraid of it.
   c) A pig goes "oink oink" and loves to take a bath in the mud.
   d) A snail is a very slow animal. It carries its house on its back.
   e) A tiger is black and yellow and is a big cat that lives in Africa.
   f) A bear can be brown, black or white and lives in the forest or on the ice.
   g) A monkey can jump from tree to tree and can make funny sounds.

2. **Which animals are meant here? Start with: *This animal is...***

   a) This animal is a bird, but it can't fly. It lives near the South Pole and can swim in the sea. It eats fish.
   b) This animal is a bird. It can fly and it sometimes repeats words that it hears.
   c) This animal has got a very big mouth and big teeth. It is green and lives in the water. It is very quiet and it can't run quickly, but it swims very fast.
   d) This animal is very big and grey. It has got a trunk and very big ears. It lives in Africa or Asia.

3. **Read the following text.**
   a. **Correct the text and write it down correctly.**
   b. **Translate your text into German.**

   Tigers are big birds. They are yellow and red. They live in England or Asia. They can fly. They can't run quickly. They usually eat bananas. Today, they aren't in danger. So lots of people don't try to save them.

4. a. **Translate the following verbs into German.**
   b. **Which verbs do you need for the sentences? Fill in.**

   a) to crawl   e) to bite
   b) to hunt   f) to bark
   c) to feed   g) to sing
   d) to climb

   a) Ich muss meinen Hund jeden Tag füttern. – to...
   b) Affen klettern gerne auf Bäume. – to...
   c) Vögel können schön singen. – to...
   d) Löwen jagen gerne andere Tiere. – to...
   e) Hunde, die bellen, beißen nicht. – to... & to...
   f) Schlangen kriechen am Boden. – to...

5. **Translate the following sentences into English.**

   a) Mein Hamster lebt in einem Käfig.
   b) Peters Hühner leben in einem Hühnerstall.
   c) Mein Hund hat eine Hundehütte im Garten.

S-genitive

Verwendung im Singular

Man benutzt ein **'s**, **s'** oder einen **Apostroph**, um über eine Sache oder Person zu reden, die jemand anderem gehört.

Handelt es sich um den Besitz einer Person im Singular, steht erst der Apostroph **'** und dann das **s**:

Beispiel: *Ben's dog is black.* – Bens Hund ist schwarz.

Verwendung im Plural (regelmäßig)

Wenn es um die regelmäßig gebildete Pluralform geht, steht erst das reguläre Plural-**s** und dann der Apostroph **'** :

Beispiel: *The Millers' house is new.* – Das Haus der Müllers ist neu.

Verwendung im Plural (unregelmäßig)

Geht es um die unregelmäßig gebildete Pluralform, steht – wie beim Singular – erst der Apostroph **'** und dann das **s**:

Beispiel: *The children's homework is wrong.* – Die Hausaufgaben der Kinder sind falsch

Verwendung bei Endungen auf ‚s'

Endet ein Name (Singular oder Plural) bereits auf ‚**s**', wird einfach ein Apostroph **'** angehängt:

Beispiel: *James' sister is very nice.* – James Schwester ist sehr nett.

S-genitive

1. **Write down what belongs to whom. Use the singular genitive.**
   For example: *Mary has got a cat. It's Mary's cat.*

   a) Jeremy has got a dog. It's...

   b) My sister has got a blue pen. It's...

   c) Paul has got a budgie. It's...

   d) The woman has got a blue car. It's...

   e) Our hamster has got a cage. It's...

   f) My dad has got a restaurant. It's...

2. **Write down what belongs to whom. Use the plural genitive.**

   a) The Connors have got a nice house. It's...

   b) The Bakers live in a nice flat. It's...

   c) The boys have got a new basketball. It's...

   d) The girls have got their own TV. It's...

   e) The twins have got new T-shirts. It's...

3. **What can you say about the following properties? Use the singular and plural genitive.**
   For example: *Peter has got a big room. – Peter's room is big.*

   a) My parents live in a small flat.

   b) Peter has got a new bike.

   c) Our friends have got a nice house.

   d) Sandra has got a crazy cat.

   e) Sally lives in a small room.

   f) The cats have got a basket in the kitchen.

   g) Our teacher has got a younger wife.

4. **Translate the following genitives into English.**

   a) Das Haus der Müllers brennt. – *The ... house is burning.*

   b) Susans Stifte sind unter dem Tisch. *... pencils are under the table.*

   c) Die Hefte der Mädchen sind in der Tasche. *The ... exercise books are under the table.*

   d) Das Auto des Lehrers ist rot. *The ... car is red.*

   e) Sallys Schwester hat schwarze Haare. *... sister has got black hair.*

At home

S-genitive

1. Write complete sentences about what belongs to whom. Start with: *This is ... / These are ...*

   a) John – sister.
   b) My sisters – new CDs
   c) Paul – budgie
   d) The women – red cars
   e) Our hamster – cage
   f) My dad – restaurants
   g) The children – English books
   h) Chris – mum.
   i) The Miller – twins

2. Look at the pictures and write down what belongs to whom. Start with:
   In picture a) you can see ...

   a)  – the Garrets
   b)  – my dad
   c)  – Miles
   d)  – the children
   e)  – mum
   f)  – Adam

3. What can you say about these people/animals?

   a) My grandparents live in a big house. – *My grandparents' house is ...*
   b) My sister has got a red car.
   c) Our teachers have got crazy clothes.
   d) Liam has got a stupid girlfriend.
   e) The Millers live in a huge house.
   f) The dogs have got a football in the garden.
   g) Our mother works in an old office.
   h) The children have got new books.
   i) Chris has got a very nice father.

4. Translate the following sentences into English. Use the genitive.

   a) Peters Mutter arbeitet nicht in einem Büro.
   b) Die Hausaufgabe der Kinder ist falsch.
   c) Die Taschen der Mädchen liegen unter dem Tisch.
   d) Das Haus der Smith ist sehr groß.
   e) Katies Bruder ist sehr nett.
   f) Die Pullover der Männer sind grün.
   g) Die Farben der Hunde sind schwarz und grau.

Food and drinks

Food and drinks

Wenn du über Lebensmittel sprechen möchtest, benötigst du einige wesentliche Vokabeln. Die wichtigsten findest du hier:

Frucht	fruit		Kuchen	cake
Apfel	apple		Brot	bread
Birne	pear		Ei	egg
Banane	banana		Fleisch	meat
Zitrone	lemon		Fisch	fish
Orange	orange		Süßigkeiten	sweets
Weintraube	grape		Suppe	soup
Kirsche	cherry		Butter	butter
Erdbeere	strawberry		Nudeln	noodles
Ananas	pineapple		Reis	rice
Pfirsich	peach			

Gemüse	vegetable		Wasser	water
Tomate(n)	tomato(es)		Saft	juice
Erbse	pea		Bier	beer
Gurke	cucumber		Wein	wine
Bohne	bean		Tee	tea
Kartoffel(n)	potato(es)		Kaffee	coffee
Karotte	carrot		Milch	milk
Salat	salad		Limonade	lemonade
Zwiebel	onion			

Meals

Frühstück	breakfast
Mittagessen	lunch
Brunch	brunch
Kaffeetrinken	teatime
Abendessen	evening meal

Phrases

Magst du ...?	Do you like...?
Ich mag nicht ...	I don't like...
Ich liebe ...	I love...
Mein Lieblingsessen ist ...	My favourite food is...

Verbs and adjectives

Wenn du über Essen und Trinken sprichst, benötigst du häufig auch bestimmte Verben und Adjektive. Hier findest du einige:

essen	to eat		köstlich	delicious
trinken	to drink		lecker	tasty
kochen	to cook		eklig	disgusting
spülen	to wash up		sauer	sour
einkaufen	to buy sth.		süß	sweet
probieren	to try		salzig	salty
backen	to bake		scharf	spicy
schmecken	to taste			
riechen	to smell			
bevorzugen	to prefer			

At home

Food and drinks

1. Translate the following words into German.

   a) apple

   b) potatoes

   c) carrot

   d) meat

   e) banana

   f) cucumber

   g) tomato

   h) sweets

2. Look at the mixed-up words. Which fruits are hidden here? Write them down.

   a) aanban

   b) tsbwyerrar

   c) reap

   d) aecph

   e) nrgaoe

   f) iaepnlpep

3. Which vegetables are meant here? Write down complete sentences.

   a) A ... is orange and rabbits like to eat it, too.

   b) A ... is very small, round and green.

   c) A ... is red and you find it in ketchup, too.

4. Translate the following sentences and questions about food into English.

   a) Magst du Fleisch?

   b) Ich mag Kartoffeln.

   c) Welches ist dein Lieblingsessen?

   d) Ich bevorzuge Reis mit Sauce.

   e) Magst du Obst?

5. Translate the following sentences into German.

   a) This soup smells very good.

   b) The meat tastes salty.

   c) I drink lemonade.

   d) My mother often cooks hot beans.

Food and drinks

1. **Translate the following words into English and write them into a chart with the categories fruit / vegetables / drinks.**

   a) Kartoffeln
   b) Apfel
   c) Karotte
   d) Limonade
   e) Banane
   f) Gurke
   g) Tomate
   h) Milch
   i) Pfirsich
   j) Weintraube
   k) Bier
   l) Bohne

2. **Look at the mixed-up words.**
   a. Which food is hidden here?
   b. Write down sentences about their colour. For example: *A lemon is yellow.*

   a) etam
   b) tsbwyerrar
   c) reap
   d) aregno jciue
   e) acek
   f) rbdae
   g) irec

3. **Translate into German. What does the sales assistant say at the market.**

   *Good morning ladies and gentlemen. Today I'm offering (dt.: anbieten) you fresh salad, green and red tomatoes, the best potatoes of the region, and I've got new beans from Germany.
   I've also got white and red onions from my farm and very big cucumbers, too.
   The fruit is very good today. I've got apples, pears, strawberries, and the best bananas you can find in town. Come here and taste my fresh peaches, too. They're delicious!*

4. **Your friend from England visits you in Germany and your mum wants to know more about his favourite food and drinks.**
   a. Translate her questions into English.
   b. Translate your friend's answers into German.

   Mother: Magst du Kartoffeln mit Fleisch oder bevorzugst du Bohnen?
   Guest: Well, I like potatoes and beans, but I don't eat meat. I like fish.

   Mother: Welches ist dein Lieblingsessen?
   Guest: Oh, my favourite food is salad and I love peas with rice and sauce.

   Mother: Magst du auch Obst?
   Guest: Yes, I love apples and pears. But strawberries are my favourite fruit.

   Mother: Isst du morgens Frühstück?
   Guest: No, I only drink a cup of tea with milk and sugar.

At home

Body parts and clothes

Body parts

Wenn du über einen Menschen sprechen möchtest, beschreibst du häufig dessen Aussehen und somit auch seinen Körper. Hier findest du die Vokabeln für die wesentlichen Körperteile des Menschen:

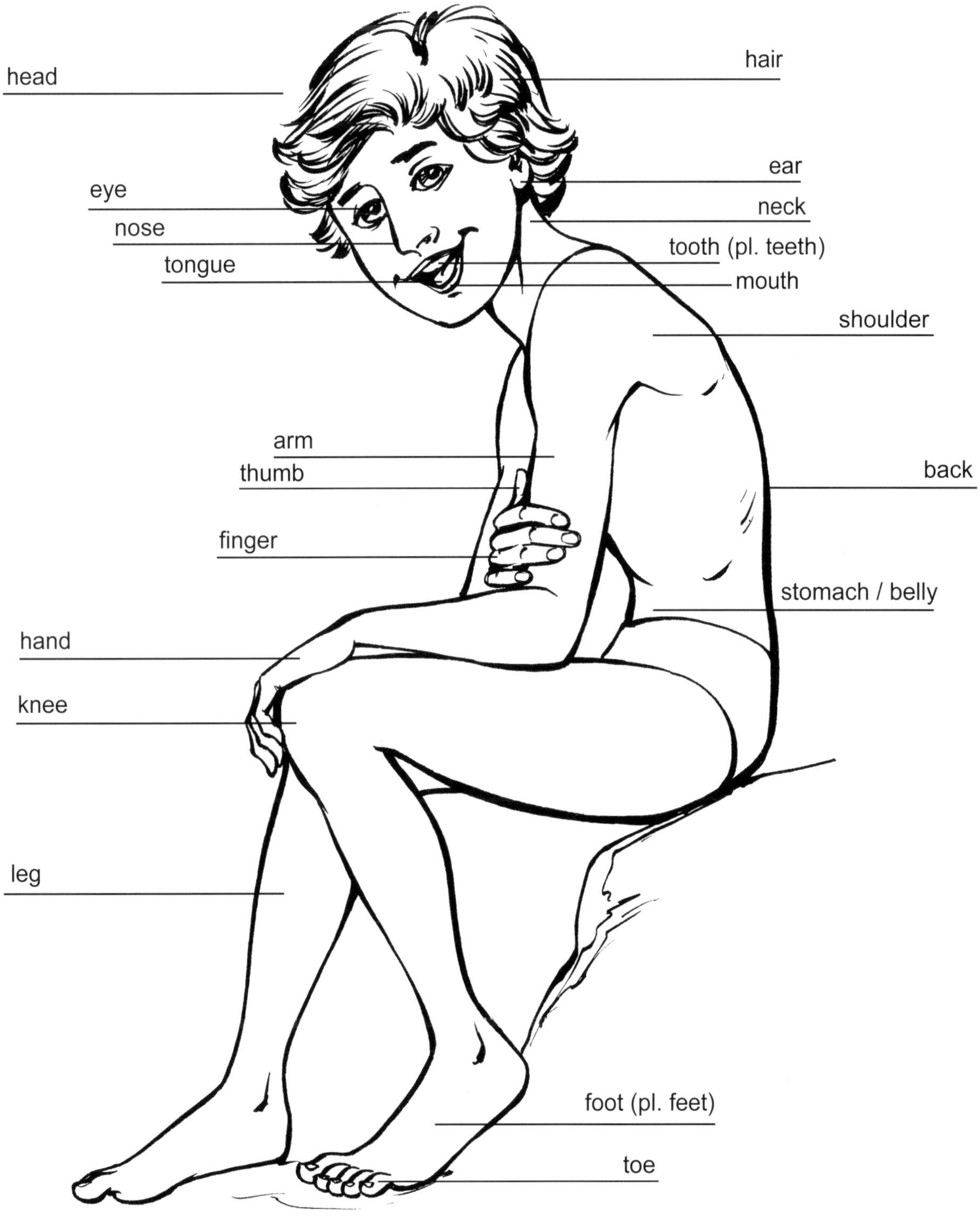

- head
- hair
- eye
- ear
- nose
- neck
- tongue
- tooth (pl. teeth)
- mouth
- shoulder
- arm
- thumb
- back
- finger
- stomach / belly
- hand
- knee
- leg
- foot (pl. feet)
- toe

At home

Body parts and clothes

Clothes

Wenn du über die Kleidung sprechen möchtest, benötigst du bestimmte Vokabeln.
Die wesentlichen findest du hier:

Jacke	*jacket*	Bikini	*bikini*
Pullover	*pullover*	Badeanzug	*bathing costume / swimsuit*
T-Shirt	*T-shirt*	Badehose	*swimming trunks*
Hemd	*shirt*	Schuh	*shoe*
Unterhemd	*vest*	Strumpfhose	*tights*
Unterhose	*underpants*	Strumpf	*sock*
Bluse	*blouse*	Schal	*scarf*
Hose	*trousers*	Mütze	*cap*
Jeans	*jeans*	Hut	*hat*
Rock	*skirt*	Handschuhe	*gloves*
Kleid	*dress*	Anzug	*suit*
Schlafanzug	*pyjama*	BH	*bra*
Gürtel	*belt*	kurze Hose	*shorts*

Verbs and adjectives

Wenn du über Kleidung und Aussehen eines Menschen sprichst, benötigst du Verben und Adjektive, um dies zu tun. Hier findest du einige der wichtigsten:

anprobieren	*to try sth. on*	weit / locker	*loose*
kaufen	*to buy*	eng	*tight*
tragen	*to wear*	klein	*small*
passen	*to fit*	groß	*big*
fragen	*to ask*	lang	*long*
nach etw. schauen	*to look for sth.*	kurz	*short*
haben	*to have (got)*	gut	*good*
aussehen	*to look*	schlecht	*bad*

At home

Body parts and clothes

1. **Translate the following parts of the body into English**

   a) Kopf
   b) Arm
   c) Hals
   d) Rücken
   e) Finger
   f) Fuß
   g) Bein
   h) Zeh

2. **What body parts are meant here?**
   Start with: *This body part is...* oder *These body parts are...*

   a) It's on your head.
   b) You've got 10 on your feet.
   c) It's the middle of your body. It's your back.
   d) You've got two and you walk with them.
   e) You've got one in your face and you eat with it.

3. **Look at the pictures and write down the body parts you see.**
   Start with: *In this picture I see…*

   a)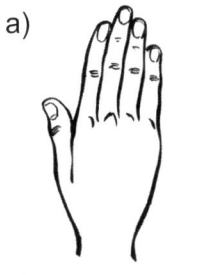
   b)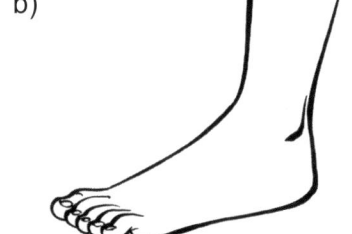
   c)
   d)
   e)
   f)

4. **What do these persons wear? Write down sentences. Start with: *Today, Sarah is wearing...***

		pullover	jeans	T-shirt	skirt	jacket	socks
a)	Sarah			✓	✓		✓
b)	Pete	✓	✓				✓
c)	Steve		✓	✓		✓	
d)	Mrs Miller	✓			✓		

5. **Translate the following sentences into English.**

   a) Heute trägt Susan ein Kleid und neue Schuhe. (to wear)
   b) Diese Schuhe passen nicht. (to fit)
   c) Dieser Bikini sieht gut aus. (to look)
   d) Mary trägt ein rotes Kleid und eine schwarze Jacke. (to wear)
   e) Unter seinem Anzug trägt Herr Smith ein weißes Hemd. (to wear)

Body parts and clothes

1. **Translate the following sentences into English.**

   a) Wie viele Finger hast du?
   b) Mein Arm ist gebrochen.
   c) Du stehst auf meinem Fuß!
   d) Er hat ein Tattoo auf dem Rücken.
   e) Marys rechtes Bein ist länger als ihr linkes Bein.
   f) Meine Freundin hat schöne weiße Zähne.
   g) Steve hat grüne Augen und braune Haare.

2. **Look at the following words.**
   a. Write descriptions about them and say where you find them.
   b. Note all the parts of your head that you know. It should be at least 8.

   a) neck
   b) fingers
   c) belly
   d) teeth
   e) nose

3. **Look at the mixed-up sentence. Find all 12 parts of the body and write them down. Translate all of them into German.**

   DNGKTOEKSLGNHANDLSNOSEMDKHAIRKDLFINGERHSNTEETHCNHDN
   MOUTHGSBXVKNEEHFKGEARJGLEEYENDFAONECKLGNADBELLYSHE

4. **Look at the following words. Translate them into English and put them into a chart with *winter* and *summer*.**

   a) T-Shirt   e) Badehose
   b) Bluse   f) Strumpfhose
   c) Schal   g) Rock
   d) Handschuhe   h) Jacke

5. **What can you say about Janet's habits? Watch the chart and write down complete English sentences. Start with:** *Janet is wearing…*

	T-Shirt	Bluse	Bikini	Gürtel	Strumpfhose	BH	Hose
tragen	lang			eng			schwarz
mögen			eng				weiß
hassen		weit			lang		
suchen	eng			lang		neu	
kaufen		eng	gelb				weit

At home

Colours

Colours

Wenn du Dinge beschreiben möchtest, benötigst du die Vokabeln für die Farben und deren Intensität.

Hier findest du die wichtigsten:

rot	*red*	hell	*light*
gelb	*yellow*	dunkel	*dark*
blau	*blue*	tief	*deep*
schwarz	*black*	blass	*pale*
weiß	*white*	pastell	*pastel*
grün	*green*		
rosa	*pink*	bunt	*colourful*
lila	*purple*		
braun	*brown*		
grau	*grey*		
orange	*orange*		
türkis	*turquoise*		
gold	*gold*		
silber	*silver*		

Verbs

Verben, die in diesem Zusammenhang von Bedeutung sein können, findest du hier:

malen	*to paint*	löschen	*to erase*
zeichnen	*to draw*	mischen	*to mix*
anstreichen	*to paint*		
radieren	*to rub out / to erase*		
färben	*to colour / to dye*		
tönen	*to tint*		

Colours

1. **Write down the following colours in German.**

   a) red
   b) green
   c) yellow
   d) blue
   e) purple

   f) black
   g) white
   h) pink
   i) grey
   j) brown

2. **Which colours do the following things have?**

   a) yellow
   b) green
   c) blue
   d) grey
   e) white
   f) purple

   1) snow
   2) sky
   3) sun
   4) grass
   5) grapes
   6) elephant

3. **Complete the following sentences with the correct colours and write them down.**

   a) Elephants are…
   b) Bees are… and…
   c) Blood is…
   d) Grass is…
   e) Snow is…

4. **Tick (✓) the right solution for the following colours.**

   a) **red**   tomato ☐   snow ☐   sun ☐
   b) **green**   taxi ☐   grass ☐   sky ☐
   c) **blue**   sunflower ☐   sea ☐   tree ☐
   d) **yellow**   wood ☐   water ☐   sun ☐
   e) **white**   snow ☐   elephant ☐   apple ☐

5. **Complete the sentences with the missing colours.**

   | blue   grey   red   green   yellow   white |

   a) The tomatoes in our garden are still ___. Mum says we can't eat them like this.
   b) It's nice to see the ___ polar bears in the zoo.
   c) When the sun shines, the sky is ___.
   d) When the lights are ___ you aren't allowed to cross the street.
   e) The German mailvans are ___.
   f) Elephants have got very big ears and they are ___.

At home

Colours

1. **Which colours do the following things have?**

   a) The sun is...
   b) An English taxi is...
   c) Snow is...
   d) The grass in our garden is...
   e) The colour of wood is...
   f) When it's raining, the sky is...
   g) The ocean is...

2. **What does Megan say about herself? Translate the text into German.**

   Hi, my name is Megan. This is our house. It's white and has got a red roof. Inside, everything is blue. My mum loves blue and green very much. My room is pink and white. I've got a red bed and a purple wardrobe. My brother's room is grey and blue. He likes dark colours. I like our colourful house very much.

3. **Find out the 9 colours in the mixed-up sentence.**
   a. Write them down in German.
   b. Fill in the English vocabulary and write down the sentences below.

   KLDNBROWNMSDLWHITELMNDPURPLENBXREDLOG
   GREENMNBLACKJNGPINKLHNYELLOWJFNGHGREY

   a) The trees in our garden have got ... leaves in summer.
   b) Apples are normally ... or ...
   c) I love the ... bananas that my mum buys every Friday.
   d) Our English taxis are ...
   e) When it snows in winter, the roof of our house is totally ...

4. **Translate the following sentences into English.**

   a) Meine Mutter kauft ein rotes Kleid mit schwarzen Punkten (dots) und graue Schuhe.
   b) In unserer Klasse gibt es viele bunte Bilder und eine rote und eine blaue Wand.
   c) Meine Lieblingsfarben sind türkis, braun und rosa.
   d) Wir mögen blaue Hosen und gelbe T-Shirts.
   e) Peter und Sam haben blaue Augen und schwarze Haare.

5. **Which solution is correct? Tick it.**

   a) A bear in the forest is
   ☐ brown
   ☐ yellow
   ☐ purple

   b) A polar bear is
   ☐ blue
   ☐ black
   ☐ white

   c) An elephant is
   ☐ red
   ☐ grey
   ☐ green

At home

Personal pronouns

Verwendung Personalpronomen (Subjekt)

Ein **Personalpronomen** dient als Ersatz für ein Nomen (Person oder Gegenstand), das als Subjekt im Satz fungiert.

Bsp.: **Peter** *is riding his bike.* → **He** *is riding his bike.*

Somit ist ein Personalpronomen ein eigenständiger Satzteil. Du benutzt ein Personalpronomen zum Beispiel immer dann, wenn du über dich selbst sprichst (selten verwendet man dann seinen Namen!).

For example: *I'm going now.*

oder wenn du jemanden direkt ansprichst:

For example: *Can **you** help me, please?*

Sprichst du über eine dritte Person, benutzt du zuerst zwar dessen Namen, verwendest dann aber meist ein Personalpronomen:

For example: *John is very nice.* ***He*** *lives in my street.*

Personalpronomen (Subjekt)

Im Englischen gibt es 7 unterschiedliche Personalpronomen **(Subjekt)**. *You* wird sowohl im Singular (du) als auch im Plural (ihr) verwendet:

ich	*I*	wir	*we*
du	*you*	ihr	*you*
er	*he*	sie	*they*
sie	*she*		
es	*it*		

Pronouns and question words

Personal pronouns

1. **Translate the following German pronouns into English.**

   a) ich

   b) du

   c) er

   d) ihr

   e) wir

   f) sie (viele)

2. **Which pronouns replace the following nouns?**

   a) Sarah

   b) Dylan and John

   c) Mary and I

   d) our dog

   e) Thomas

3. **Write down the sentences by filling in a pronoun.**

   a) My name is Sarah. ___ am from London.

   b) Look at the picture. This is my father. ___ is 45 years old.

   c) Linda is my mum. ___ is a teacher.

   d) These are my brother Jimmy and my sister Jane. ___ are twins and ___ are 12 years old.

   e) Our dog is a boy, Bob. ___ is very funny

   f) ___ all live in London. ___ is the capital of England.

   g) My grandparents don't live here. ___ live in Edinburgh.

4. **Write down the following text and fill in the missing pronouns.**

it (2x)	she (1x)	he (1x)	I (3x)	we (1x)	they (1x)

   _____ is a nice day today. My best friend Peter and _____ are going out to play football. _____ meet some other friends in the park. _____ are waiting for us there. _____ like football very much. _____ is my favourite sport. My mum likes football, too. _____ is a good football player. Dad isn't at work today. _____ will come to the park, too. My friends and I, _____ play football until the sun goes down. My mother says that _____ must be home by 6 o'clock. My friend Tom (_____ is only 10 years old) must be home by 5 o'clock.

5. **Replace the names with the correct pronouns.**

   a) Ben is my best friend.

   b) Jim and I are going to the swimming pool after school.

   c) Look, our cat is lying in the sun.

   d) Mum and dad watch TV in the evening.

   e) I think Charlotte is a very nice girl.

Personal pronouns

1. **Fill in the correct pronouns.**

   a) Amy is a nice girl. ... lives next to my house.
   b) Pete lives in London. ... is my best friend.
   c) Mandy and I often go to an Italian restaurant. ... love the pasta there.
   d) "Do ... like pop music?"
   e) "How old are you?" "Oh, ... am 10."
   f) "Where is your dog?" "... is in the garden, I think."

2. **Translate the German sentences into English. Replace the nouns with the correct pronouns.**

   a) Lucas ist im Garten.
   b) Emily und ihre Eltern sind sehr nett.
   c) Jerry und ich machen unsere Hausaufgaben.
   d) Der Hund spielt im Haus.
   e) Mama und Papa schauen fern.

3. **Which pronouns replace the following people? Write down the sentences using the pronouns.**

   a) Jake and Sally are sitting in the living room.
   b) The hamster runs around in the cage.
   c) My little brother is crazy.
   d) Can Sarah and Jane swim?
   e) Does Ellie like ice cream?
   f) What does Callum do in the kitchen?
   g) The kids are sitting in the classroom.
   h) Our teacher and I are cleaning the board.

4. **Translate the following sentences into English.**

   a) Du bist sehr hübsch.
   b) Sie sitzen im Wohnzimmer.
   c) Sie schaut fern.
   d) Wir haben Hunger.
   e) Du kommst zu spät.
   f) Ich mache meine Hausaufgaben.
   g) Er lernt seine Vokabeln.

5. **Write down the following text using the correct pronouns to fill in the gaps.**

   _____ is a very nice day today. The sun is shining and _____ is very hot. My best friends and _____ are playing in the garden. _____ are playing volleyball. _____ like football very much but the girls, _____ prefer volleyball. My dad is in the kitchen. _____ is preparing lunch. Mum is at work. _____ is a nurse in the hospital. _____ is a very big hospital in town and _____ often comes home late in the evening. My sister Sally and my brother John are in the garden, too. _____ are playing hockey. Our cat Mimmi is sleeping under a tree. _____ is very tired, _____ think. Our dog, who hasn't yet got a name, is in the garden, too. _____ is playing with a ball.

Pronouns and question words

Possessive pronouns

Verwendung Possessivpronomen

Ein Possessivpronomen ersetzt besitzanzeigende Nomen, also solche Dinge, die in einem Besitz stehen oder zu etwas / jemandem gehören.

    Bsp.: *This is **Peter's** car.* ➔ *This is **his** car.*

Im Deutschen entspricht dies der Frage nach **wessen?** oder **wem?**

Du verwendest ein solches Possessivpronomen immer dann, wenn du z. B. in einer Erzählung nicht ständig den Namen der betreffenden Person wiederholen möchtest.

Bsp.:
- *This is **Peter's** car. **Peter's** car is red. **Peter's** car is big...*
- *This is **Peter's** car. **His** car is red and **his** car is big...*

Possessivpronomen

Im Englischen gibt es 7 unterschiedliche Possessivpronomen. *Your* wird sowohl im Singular (dein/e) als auch im Plural (ihr/e) verwendet:

mein/e	*my*	unser/e	*our*
dein/e	*your*	euer/eure	*your*
sein/e	*his*	ihr/e	*their*
ihr/e	*her*		
sein/ihr	*its*		

Possessive pronouns

1. **Write down the following pronouns in English.**

   a) mein/e   d) ihr/e   g) euer/eure

   b) dein/e   e) sein/ihr (neutr.)   h) ihr/e

   c) sein/e   f) unser/e

2. **Fill in the correct pronouns and write down complete sentences.**

   a) I need ... (meinen) computer today.

   b) Do you know where ... (deine) trousers are?

   c) We are closing ... (unsere) books now.

   d) He washes ... (sein) hair every second day.

   e) I want ... (meine) books back.

   f) The Smiths are painting ... (ihr) fences green.

   g) Mary-Lou, are ... (deine) parents at home?

   h) She tidies up ... (ihr) room every Saturday.

   i) We love ... (unsere) dog.

3. **Fill in the correct pronouns.**

   a) Next Christmas, I'll get ____ new computer.

   b) Holly, where are ____ bikes? I can't find them.

   c) Riley has got a little brother.—What's ____ name?

   d) I am very happy: ____ best friend lives in my street.

   e) Hey Judy, Ethan loves ____.

   f) Samuel? Carrie? ____ mother is calling.

4. **Translate the following sentences into English.**

   a) Mein Auto ist gelb.

   b) Ich mag deine Augen.

   c) Seine Eltern sind zu Hause.

   d) Ihre Katzen schlafen gerade.

   e) Sein (des Hundes) Ball ist im Garten.

   f) Unsere Lehrer sind sehr nett.

   g) Ist euer Haus weiß?

   h) Ihre Fahrräder sind hinter dem Haus.

Pronouns and question words

Possessive pronouns

1. Write down the pronouns in German. Take care with their meanings.

    a) my
    b) your
    c) his
    d) her
    e) its
    f) our
    g) their

2. Read the following sentences.
    a. Fill in the correct pronouns.
    b. Translate the sentences into German.

    a) I love ... little brother very much. He is very cute.

    b) Do you know where ... parents are? I can't find them.

    c) We're looking for ... books. They aren't on the table.

    d) She washes ... hair every morning.

    e) I brush ... teeth twice: In the morning and in the evening.

    f) They are painting ... houses red because they like the colour very much.

    g) Lucy, are ... sisters at home? They don't answer the phone.

    h) He does ... homework every day at 2 o'clock.

    i) We love ... cat. It's black and very beautiful.

3. Replace the underlined words with pronouns.
    a. Write down the sentences.
    b. Translate the sentences into German.

    a) Look, this is <u>Sarah's and my</u> book.

    b) <u>Jerry's</u> father is a police officer.

    c) <u>Chloe's</u> mother lives in New York.

    d) This is <u>my dog's</u> ball.

    e) <u>John's and Katie's</u> teachers are very nice.

    f) Is this <u>Gerry's</u> football?

    g) Are <u>Katherine's</u> parents at home?

    h) <u>Tom's, Joshua's and my bikes</u> are red and green.

4. Übersetze die folgenden Sätze ins Englische.

    a) Meine Autos sind blau und gelb.

    b) Ich mag deine Augen und ihre Haare.

    c) Seine Eltern sind zu Hause.

    d) Seine Hunde schlafen gerade auf ihrem (Jaydens und Sandras) Bett.

    e) Sein (des Hamsters) Käfig ist in meinem Zimmer.

    f) Eure Lehrer sind besser als unsere Lehrer.

    g) Ist unsere Mutter zu Hause?

    h) Ihr (Mirandas) Fahrrad ist hinter deinem Haus.

Object pronouns

Verwendung Objektpronomen

Ein solches Pronomen dient als Ersatz für ein Objekt (Person oder Gegenstand) im Satz.

Bsp.: *Peter loves **Sarah**.* → *He loves **her**.*

Im Deutschen entspricht dies dem **Akkusativobjekt** (**wen** oder **was?**).

Du verwendest ein solches Objektpronomen immer dann, wenn du z. B. in einer Erzählung nicht ständig den Namen der betreffenden Person oder des Gegenstandes wiederholen möchtest.

Bsp.:
- *Peter loves **Sarah**. He likes **Sarah** very much. He meets **Sarah** every day.*

- *Peter loves **Sarah**. He likes **her** very much and meets **her** every day.*

Objektpronomen

Im Englischen gibt es 7 unterschiedliche Objektpronomen. *You* wird sowohl im Singular (dich) als auch im Plural (euch) verwendet:

mich	*me*	uns	*us*
dich	*you*	euch	*you*
ihn	*him*	sie	*them*
sie	*her*		
es	*it*		

Object pronouns

1. **Translate the following pronouns into English.**

    a) ihn
    b) sie (Sing.)
    c) euch
    d) uns
    e) sie (Pl.)
    f) dich
    g) mich
    h) es

2. **Write down correct sentences by using pronouns to fill in the gaps.**

    a) Take the apples and put ... into the basket under the tree.
    b) Where is your mother? I want to talk to ...
    c) We are hungry. Give ... something to eat, please.
    d) Daniel is my best friend. I like ... very much.
    e) Do you know where my books are? I can't find ...
    f) Where is the hamster? I can't find ...
    g) I'm thirsty. Please, give ... some water.
    h) I can't come to your party on Friday, but here is a little present for ...
    i) This is a nice dress. I like ... very much.
    j) Look at ...! Isn't she beautiful?

3. **Underline the parts of the sentences that can be replaced by a pronoun and replace them. For example:** *Talk to <u>Mary-Ann</u>.* ➔ *Talk to her.*

    a) Talk to your sister.
    b) Listen to your father.
    c) I'm looking for my English book.
    d) Please shut the window.
    e) I can't find my books.
    f) Leave the door open, please.
    g) I like Henry and George very much.
    h) I meet Myra after school.
    i) Gina is talking to her uncle.
    j) Can you help me and Harry?
    k) Please open your book.
    l) I eat bananas every day.
    m) I can't write this postcard.

4. **Translate the following sentences into English.**

    a) Ich mag dich.
    b) Er trifft uns nach der Schule.
    c) Sie ruft mich am Nachmittag an.
    d) Sie essen es nicht.

Object pronouns

1. **Write down the following sentences using the correct pronouns.**

    a) I like Jack. Do you like ..., too?
    b) I go to school with Sandy. Do you know ...?
    c) Liam, Thomas, I really like ...
    d) My teacher always gives me good marks. I think, she likes ...
    e) John and Malcom are nice boys. I like ... very much.
    f) I love football. Do you like ..., too?
    g) Ruby: Jim, I love ...
    h) Our neighbours always shout at my brother and me. I think they don't like ...

2. **Write down sentences and use the correct pronouns.**
    For example: *look – Sarah*   →   **Look at <u>her</u>!**

    a) put – apples – into the basket
    b) I – talk to – mother
    c) Give – Archie and me – something to eat, please
    d) I – like – Oscar – very much
    e) I – can't find – my books
    f) I – am looking for – hamster
    g) I'm thirsty. Give – I – some water.
    h) I – like – new dress very much
    i) Look at – Charlotte and Isabelle. Aren't they beautiful?

3. **Read the following sentences.**
    a. **Replace the underlined parts with a pronoun.**
    b. **Translate the "new" sentences into German.**

    a) Look at <u>Grace</u>.
    b) Listen to <u>Max</u>.
    c) I'm looking for <u>my book</u>.
    d) Please shut <u>the door</u>.
    e) I can't find <u>my keys</u>.
    f) Leave <u>the window</u> open, please.
    g) I like <u>James and Sam</u> very much.
    h) I meet <u>Mrs Smith</u> after school.
    i) Mary is talking to <u>Jim</u>.
    j) Can you help <u>me and my brother</u>?
    k) Please open <u>the door</u>.
    l) I eat <u>apples</u> every day.
    m) I can't write <u>this text</u>.

4. **Translate the following sentences into English.**

    a) Ich spreche mit ihr und dann mit ihm.
    b) Er ruft dich an und besucht uns später.
    c) Sie kennt mich sehr gut.
    d) Hör mir zu, ich esse sie nicht.

Pronouns and question words

Question words

Fragewörter Verwendung

Im Englischen gibt es zahlreiche Fragewörter, die dazu dienen, gezielt nach bestimmten Dingen / Personen zu fragen.
Viele dieser Fragwörter beginnen mit „wh".

Die Fragewörter stehen in der Regel am Satzanfang.

Beispiel: *Where is our house?*
What's your name?
Why are you too late?

Fragewörter

Die folgenden Fragewörter sind die Geläufigsten in der englischen Sprache:

was	*what*
wann	*when*
wo	*where*
warum	*why*
wer	*who*
wessen	*whose*
welche/r/s	*which*
wie	*how*

Pronouns and question words

Question words

1. **Translate the following question words into English.**

   a) was?
   b) wann?
   c) wo?
   d) warum?
   e) wer?
   f) wie?

2. **Fill in the correct question words and write down complete questions.**

   who   where   why   how   what   when

   a) ... is your best friend? – It's Marc.
   b) ... do you come from? – I come from New York.
   c) ... is your favourite movie? – My favourite movie is "Ghost".
   d) ... old are you? – I am 13 years old.
   e) ... do you laugh? – I laugh because Sarah looks so funny today.
   f) ... do we write the test? – We write the test at 10 o'clock.
   g) ... is your cat? – It's in the kitchen.
   h) ... will you have? – I'll have a cup of tea, please.

3. **Tick the right solution for asking about the underlined words.**

   a) Sunny is Mary's mother.   ☐ where ☐ who

   b) We meet there at 3 o'clock.   ☐ what ☐ when

   c) We live in Maryland.   ☐ why ☐ where

   d) She'll fall off because she can't ride a bike.   ☐ why ☐ when

   e) I'm fine, thanks.   ☐ what ☐ how

4. **Translate the following questions into English.**

   a) Wer wohnt in dem roten Haus?
   b) Was isst du gerade?
   c) Wo wohnst du?
   d) Wie alt bist du?
   e) Wann treffen wir uns?
   f) Warum rufst du mich an?
   g) Wer kennt Robbie?
   h) Was machst du gerade?
   i) Wo ist mein Englischbuch?

Pronouns and question words

Question words

1. **Translate the following questions into English. Take care with the question words.**

   a) Was passiert gerade? d) Warum fragst du? g) Wessen Haus ist das?
   b) Wann kommt er? e) Wer ist sie? h) Welches Buch liest du?
   c) Wo wohnt er? f) Wie als bist du?

2. **Write down the questions using the correct question words.**

   a) Wer? – Ava is my best friend.
   b) Woher? – I come from Manchester
   c) Was – My favourite hobby is football.
   d) Wie – I am 12 years old.
   e) Warum – I'm crying because I can't find my sister.
   f) Wann – We meet at 6 o'clock in the evening.
   g) Wo – The dog is in the garden.
   h) Was – I want some cheesecake, please!

3. **Ask for the underlined part of the sentence.**

   a) <u>Daniel</u> is my best friend.
   b) I go to school at <u>7 o'clock</u>.
   c) We live in <u>London</u>.
   d) She will get a bad mark <u>because she can't speak French</u>.
   e) I am <u>fine</u>, thanks.
   f) Jessica and Lewis will meet <u>at 2 o'clock at the bus station</u>.
   g) I want <u>some hamburgers</u>, please.
   h) These are <u>Joseph's shoes</u>.
   i) <u>The red ones</u> are Carol's pullovers.

4. **Translate the following questions into English.**

   a) Wer möchte den Kuchen probieren?
   b) Was isst du gerade?
   c) Woher kommst du?
   d) Wie heißt du?
   e) Wann treffen wir uns?
   f) Wessen Adresse brauchst du?
   g) Warum rufst du mich nicht an?
   h) Wessen Auto ist Peters?
   i) Was machst du gerade?
   j) Wo und wann treffen wir uns heute Nachmittag?
   k) Wessen Schuhe stehen in der Küche?
   l) Wie viele Arbeiten / Tests schreiben wir in Englisch?

Alle Unterrichtsmaterialien
der Verlage Auer, AOL-Verlag und PERSEN

jederzeit online verfügbar

lehrerbuero.de
Jetzt kostenlos testen!

» lehrerbüro
Das Online-Portal für Unterricht und Schulalltag!